The Constructions of the East in Western Travel Narratives, 1200 CE to 1800 CE

This book investigates how the idea of the 'east' emerged in western travel narratives between the 13th and the 18th centuries. Sifting through critical travel narratives – real and imagined – it locates the changing geography as well as the perceptions surrounding India. The author presents how historical stereotypes interacted with a burgeoning demand for travelogues during this period and have fed into the way we think about Asia in general, and India in particular. From the mythical travels of Prester John to the enigmatic 'adventures' of Marco Polo, from the fraught voyages of Johannes Plano de Carpini to the missionary zeal of Friar Odoric of Pordenone and William of Rubruquis, this volume traces the history of the 'Orient' as it was understood by the west.

A major intervention in understanding how popular narratives shape history, this book will be of great interest to scholars and researchers of history, medieval history, history of travel, world literature, postcolonial studies, and general readers interested in travel narratives.

Radhika Seshan retired as Professor and Head, Department of History, Savitribai Phule Pune University (formerly University of Pune), India in July 2019, and is now Visiting Professor at the Symbiosis School of Liberal Arts, Pune. She has several publications including *Trade and Politics on the Coromandel Coast: Seventeenth to Early Eighteenth Centuries* (2012) and *Ideas and Institutions in Medieval India: Eighth to Eighteenth Centuries* (2013), as well as various edited volumes.

The Constructions of the East in Western Travel Narratives, 1200 CE to 1800 CE

Radhika Seshan

LONDON AND NEW YORK

First published 2020
by Routledge
2 Park Square, Milton Park, Abingdon, Oxon OX14 4RN

and by Routledge
52 Vanderbilt Avenue, New York, NY 10017

Routledge is an imprint of the Taylor & Francis Group, an informa business

© 2020 Radhika Seshan

The right of Radhika Seshan to be identified as author of this work has been asserted by her in accordance with sections 77 and 78 of the Copyright, Designs and Patents Act 1988.

All rights reserved. No part of this book may be reprinted or reproduced or utilised in any form or by any electronic, mechanical, or other means, now known or hereafter invented, including photocopying and recording, or in any information storage or retrieval system, without permission in writing from the publishers.

Trademark notice: Product or corporate names may be trademarks or registered trademarks, and are used only for identification and explanation without intent to infringe.

British Library Cataloguing-in-Publication Data
A catalogue record for this book is available from the British Library

Library of Congress Cataloging-in-Publication Data
A catalog record for this book has been requested

ISBN: 978-1-138-36741-8 (hbk)
ISBN: 978-0-367-80915-7 (ebk)

Typeset in Sabon
by Apex CoVantage, LLC

For my family

Contents

Acknowledgements		viii
Introduction		1
1	The imagined lands	11
2	Locating the east	22
3	Exploring the east	38
4	Defining the east	51
5	Recasting the east	69
6	Anchoring the 'Orient'	83
Select Bibliography		98
Index		103

Acknowledgements

This book has taken an inordinately long time to complete, for I first began work on it over ten years ago. It has been an ambitious project, and has involved many people, as well as a great deal of reading (which last was fun but having to organise my ideas was not!).

As always, thanks are due to many people. My daughters, Nisha and Varsha, have regularly been roped in as editors and as audience, as well as sounding boards as and when required. The last version was read through by Varsha, who pointed out the inconsistencies of both argument and tense and made sure I explained things more coherently. My sister, who came to visit me, was also roped in to read and tell me if what I had written made sense. My cousin told me that she got stuck on the first sentence and made sure I changed it. Shweta, as always, has been audience, sounding board, and tech expert.

And thanks to my friends, who asked me at regular intervals how long I was going to sit on the book without publishing it.

Radhika Seshan

Introduction

> It is accounted a romantic thing to wander among strangers and to eat their bread by the camp-fires of the other half of the world. . . . Wandering in itself is merely a form of self-indulgence. If it adds not to the stock of human knowledge, or if it gives not to others the imaginative possession of some part of the world, it is a pernicious habit. . . . It is only the wonderful traveller who sees a wonder, and only five travellers in the world's history have seen wonders. The others have seen birds and beasts, rivers and wastes, the earth and the (local) fulness thereof.

So declared the Introduction to *The Travels of Marco Polo*,[1] in the version that was printed in English in 1818.

> For anything to which a man is accustomed long, commonly grows unpleasant; whereas Variety delights him, and rescues his imagination from the tediousness of ordinary Objects. Hence is the desire men have naturally to Travaile: and though it withdraws one from his relations and country, and exposeth him to several incommodities and perils, yet the pleasure of his Voiage preponderates all apprehensions, and renders all discouragements contemptible and vain. And as there is Pleasure in Travailing, so it hath in my judgement its Utility likewise, and its Profit as well as Diversion.
> – Guy Miège,[2] a Frenchman who accompanied the Earl of Carlisle on a diplomatic mission to the court of the Tsar in 1663.

A common feature of today's world is the ubiquitous map on phones, tablets, etc. The map gives you directions from place a to place b, in the shortest possible time, and by the route which has the least traffic. But what about the world in which such devices did not exist? How did people learn about other places, perhaps located not so far away? Were these worlds real or imagined? Who went there? And how? And what did they see there? These are the questions that have resulted in travel narratives of many kinds – the 'traveller's tale'. Tales of travel could take an individual anywhere he or she wanted, in imagination, but he or she needed first to have something to grasp, which had to come through the story of someone who had 'been there, done that'.

Travel has always fascinated humans. Whether this is a genetic inheritance from the days of the nomads, or a later development from the days of more settled life, when travel was (perhaps) a way to escape the tedium of daily life, or just a desire to impress one's fellow men with one's worldly wisdom and knowledge, the fact is that travel has always been a major part of human experience. This fascination has found expression in storytelling and later in writing of all kinds. These stories could be real or imaginary and could be understood as either; but crucial to the telling of the tale is the need to make it in some sense identifiable. A tale has to have a location, and that location has to be believable, and perhaps, at a later stage, verifiable.

Storytelling is of different kinds, in both prose and poetry. This would include mythologies, oral narratives which often collapse time and space (or on the other hand locate them very firmly),[3] bardic compositions and histories, and perhaps, in a slightly later time, more 'factual' narratives. Stories have a wide audience, and the more popular a story, the greater its reach. The most popular stories are those that talk of epic battles, with the hero winning against all odds, or those that throw into sharp relief the frailties or pride of those in power. Thus, for example, we have the stories of Sindbad the Sailor, or versions of the stories from the Arabian Nights. Fables, too, are stories, and many such stories are to be found in different cultures, as can be seen in, for example, the common themes found in the Mulla Nasruddin stories, or the Birbal and Tenali Raman[4] stories in India.

The reverse can also be said to hold good, for as Romila Thapar[5] has pointed out, the retelling of a story also provides information about the context of a particular way of retelling. In other words, the story has multiple temporal and spatial locations. We can also see travel literature in this fashion for, transcending time and space, these stories continue to be read. What is read into the narrative would then belong to a different time and a different context from the one in which it was written. It is in this sense that this book deals with travel accounts.

Travel writing in the western world can perhaps be said to have come into its own from the medieval period. The medieval world was one that was circumscribed in many ways, physical and mental, and the one who transcended these restraints was someone to be regarded with awe. The travelling minstrel, the troubadour who sang of love and war, or the family bard, all were people who had a certain cachet, as having seen the world. More importantly, what they wrote (or sang) was regarded as the final word: at least until the next, more authoritative, word came along. These subsequent works were based on the earlier, which had laid down the fundamentals of the familiar. This familiar could be modified, but the essential character of 'difference' was always maintained. A traveller's tale could also in a sense be a re-affirmation of certain stereotypes, which, in the time of original composition, served perhaps to differentiate, and then became a kind of shorthand, where the explanation of difference was no longer needed, for the stereotype was firmly established.[6]

The utility of a travelogue as an account and as a source for history has been accepted for a very long time. In English, the Hakluyt Voyage volumes began to be published as early as the 16th century, and in the 19th century, there were translations into English of travelogues in different languages, all of which were seen as necessary for the reconstruction of the history of the Europeans in India. But it should be remembered that India has long attracted a range of travellers, from the Buddhist pilgrims of earlier times, to those who came to explore the possibilities of trade and then to perhaps settle in the country, to others like the celebrated al-Beruni, who famously talked of the "eye of the observer [which] apprehends the substance of that which is observed",[7] to the more recent tourist, exploring the heritage of India. In 1908, E.F. Oaten in his book *European Travellers in India*[8] declared that he would include in his work only those who had left some record of their travels, whether they were professional travellers, or those who travelled only because of the nature of their work. This still left him with a vast selection of works from which to choose.

While this book focuses on travel accounts of an earlier period, the fascination with the genre of travel writing can be seen to have continued into contemporary times as well.[9] As the tourist industry expanded and as travel began to be 'sold', travel literature too began to be studied. A special edition of the *Comparative Critical Studies* of 2007[10] begins by saying that literature tests and transgresses the boundaries of community. It goes on to say that the symbiosis between travel and fiction emerged "with the turn to modernity, before which the charge of travel liar was the bugbear of every travel writer".[11]

Travel literature may have acquired greater acceptance from the 18th century onwards, but it should be remembered that travel itself and the account of the travel – whether real or imaginary – has always had an audience. The experience of the journey is personal, but it has the potential to be shared. We are all fascinated by stories which take us out of our own lives, at least for a while. So, the travel narrative allows the armchair (or fireside) traveller to share vicariously in the thrills of the travellers' own experiences. The teller of a story has traditionally had an important place among humans, as has the eyewitness. The combination of the traveller, storyteller, and eyewitness is bound to be someone who enjoys a status often denied to others, for he or she is one who can comment with authority on that which he or she has seen, but which others have not. It is, therefore, a first-hand, eyewitness account, necessarily carrying greater credibility. However, this credibility has to be established – and so, all travellers and storytellers often use certain tropes, which help their audience to locate themselves and the story that is being told. The story of the unfamiliar has to be couched in terms of the familiar, and then extended beyond that familiar. For example, if one were to take the Sindbad stories, the 'familiar' is to be found in the stories of the voyages to a real place, India, but that land is strange, and so peopled by strange creatures, like the roc. Fantasy or fable may play a part in the tale, but there is of course a difference between a purely imaginary tale of fantasy such as those in the Arabian Nights, and the account of the traveller, such as those discussed in this book. This difference is, again, because of experience – so, the traveller is one who has experienced, and passes on that experience to others. The traveller's tale is therefore both a 'tale' – a story – and an 'account' – one that is factual (more or less) and broadly verifiable.

Within the broad genre, there are many different kinds of writing. For example, there is an entire range which examines the ways in which certain places are described, or looks at the ways in which travel and tourism began to grow into a major industry in the modern world. An example of this would be the many Lonely Planet books, the Michelin guides, or in an earlier time the Baedeker guides.[12] Another aspect of the study of travel writings has been the focus on veracity and verifiability. This has been particularly true of the study of such writing in history. Yet another branch has looked at the links between works of fiction which purport to be travelogues, such as *Gulliver's Travels* or *Robinson Crusoe*, and then to examine how such works were accepted as genuine, i.e., the social reception of such literature. Science fiction such as the works of H.G. Wells' *The Time Machine*, Jules Verne's *20,000 Leagues under the Sea*, Herman Melville's *Moby Dick* or Douglas Adams' *A Hitchhiker's Guide to the Galaxy* are all forms of travel writing. Science fiction is not commonly regarded as being part of travel narratives, for they are a genre in themselves. But they do describe time, space, the collapsing of both, and, like the more 'recognised' travelogues of Robinson Crusoe, the stories are anchored in defined landscapes even if not geographically anchored ones. While this work has not looked at such travelogues, they remain an area that needs to be explored. Finally, in recent times, the travel and tourism industry has sparked a fresh interest in modalities of travel and the study of travel in different historical periods. Today, travel and tourism is a major industry and an important part of many academic circles as well.[13] One needs only to take a quick look at the academic syllabi of travel and tourism courses to see this. This interest has expanded into many diverse fields including publishing (for example the Oxford University series on *Monumental Legacy* published between 2002 and 2012) or films such as the now iconic *Star Trek* or the *Lord of the Rings*. All have in various forms addressed the themes of travel.

A fascination with travel in general and India in particular was a prominent feature of the post-Renaissance European world, and can, in some form, be seen even today.[14] Michael Fisher's work, *Beyond the Three Seas: Travellers' Tales from Mughal India*,[15] was specifically concerned with the ways in which Europeans described the Mughal world that they were beginning to know from the 16th century onwards. An earlier work which continues to be of tremendous importance is Donald Lach's *Asia in the Making of Europe*,[16] a multivolume work which has been the starting (and often ending) point for both students of history and lay readers. The subject of foreign travel, especially of westerners travelling to the east, is one that continues to attract considerable attention.[17] Another relevant work is that of Percy G. Adams, for he has highlighted one aspect of travel writing, that which he has called the 'travel lies'.[18]

The idea of the travel lie is rooted in the fact that travel carries with it much baggage, and not just of the material variety. One part of this baggage is truth. Percy G. Adams has argued that in the Dublin edition of *Gulliver's Travels* "Jonathan Swift knowingly or unknowingly [introduced] posterity to the three kinds of travel books of the eighteenth century." These three kinds were the true travel accounts of perhaps the Ralph Fitch[19] variety, the imaginary voyage such as those of Swift himself, or in the 19th-century Jules Verne's *20,000 Leagues under the Sea*; and what Adams has called the 'travel lies'.

A travel lie (or a travel liar) would essentially be one that stretched the bounds of credibility. But these bounds would require some kind of authentication or verification before the accounts could authoritatively be dismissed as lies. Robinson Crusoe on his island was soon known to be a work of fiction, but Mandeville's Travels were understood as genuine and were not included in the category of travel lies until very much later, probably not till the 20th century. We could also look at the legends surrounding the land of Prester John. This was a mythical land, but one which acquired a great deal of credence by being rooted within a believable structure, enough that many people searched for it, and some even claimed to have found it. What I am therefore arguing is that such accounts of travel in many ways created a 'known' world, or perhaps a knowable world, which could be visited, described, and then dismissed as fabrication or accepted as genuine.

I have earlier argued that another way of describing travel accounts is to put them into three broad categories – of travel for adventure, travel for profit and travel for knowledge.[20] If studied in this fashion, Mandeville could be seen as representative of the first category, of travel for adventure, Peter Mundy the second, and Dr Helenus Scot the third. These also represent different times, for Mandeville is of the 14th century, Mundy the early 17th, and Scot the late 18th. Thus, there is a change visible not just in the genre of writing, but also in the reason for travel. Where earlier travels were to (perhaps) have an 'adventure' or know more about the world in which they lived, later travels were more concerned with accuracy in knowledge. An additional point that needs to be made is that the search for knowing could go in many different directions: to mapping as cartography, to providing maps of fictional lands – Narnia or Middle Earth; travel as search for some kind of a promised land – El Dorado, Shangri-la, or the Holy Grail; or science fiction of the H.G. Wells or the Jules Verne variety. Or perhaps we should just follow Adams himself who, quoting from the *Gentlemen's Magazine* of 1741 says that "a white Lie is that which is not intended to injure any Body in his Fortune, Interest, or Reputation but only to gratify a garrulous Disposition and the Itch of amusing People by telling them wonderful stories."[21] It is some of these 'wonderful stories', along with the more mundane travel accounts out of Europe to the 'eastern worlds' from the 13th century onwards, with which this book is concerned.

The fascination of the metaphor of travel can also be found in many other areas which seem to have no direct link to travel. The symbolism of travel for the life-cycle of human beings has been used over and over again, whether by Sufi mystics with their concept of *'safar'*,[22] as a journey towards self-realisation, which caters for many detours or halts on the way, or by John Bunyan in *The Pilgrim's Progress*, which is an allegorical tale of the search for salvation. We find this in Shakespeare also – as, for example, in the often misquoted 'journeys end in lovers' meetings'. The point that I am trying to make is that there is a clear structure to both travel and to the account of the travel – there has to be a start, the journey itself, with halts on the way, and then the return. The halts and the return are as much to be celebrated as the journey itself.

Safar is linear, for it ends in self-realisation; but travel is cyclical, because one has to return to the point of origin. Can one then argue that what changes in this cycle is the mode of representation because of the perception of the traveller? The mystic in search of the destination has to travel, but he also follows in the footsteps of those who went earlier. There are therefore markers along the way, sometimes recognisable, but often not. But what if these markers become more universally recognisable? Would they not then become tropes of identification? For example, many of the accounts describing land journeys across Asia mention having passed close by or having been told about the mountain where the 'old man of the mountain' lived. No attempt is made to explain who the old man was, or to describe him and his followers, but references to this old man, or to the mountain where he lived, are to be found even in the early 16th century, in the account of the Portuguese traveller Ludovico di Varthema. The 'old man' could be located in a vaguely Biblical land, or in the better-known land of the 'assassins', who were believed to have followed the precepts and instructions of the old man of the mountains; the point is that everyone 'knew' the old man of the mountains. How do these stereotypes add to or detract from the account? Even more, does anything change when a stereotype is later used as a form of shorthand? This is one of the questions that I hope to raise in this book, specifically the question of *'the east'*. What is the east, and what does *'the east'* become shorthand for? Such shorthand as a quick and convenient way of writing incorporates within it many symbols. In a travel account, what were the symbols that were used, what were the methods of representation and what were the processes by which such descriptions came to be representative rather than descriptive?

Another concern of this work is with the way in which some stereotypes began to acquire wider currency. They began to form the basis of the perception of difference, and such perceptions sometimes found their way into colonial perceptions. What was clear from a very early age was the idea of the east as 'different'. Difference lay in many things – in weather, in customs, in religions, and perhaps, most importantly, in perceptions of political and social systems. The travellers studied here drew the attention of their audience to all these aspects, thus highlighting the difference. It is not my intention to argue that perception of difference was automatically, or from the beginning, also a perception of the 'other' as inferior; but identification of the first could lead, in the colonial context, to the latter. This work is, therefore, an attempt to trace the way/s in which the perception of the 'east' was shaped through the travellers' accounts between the 13th and the 18th centuries. Perhaps in keeping with the travel accounts themselves, or at least those studied here, the 'east' is also narrowed down, finally, to India. This is due partly to convenience, partly to the accounts selected for study which have been restricted to those available in English, and partly to the position India occupied in western imagination from fairly early times.

The east was, through much of the period under review, not a fixed location, even if it had already become more or less located in Asia. Still, even in the middle of the 17th century, the account of Guy Miège, who went with the official English mission to the court of the Czar, said that he was in the east as soon as he crossed the Volga. For him the east was not in Asia but was to be found east of *his* world.

While the ways in which the east was constructed and defined are discussed, this work is not directly concerned with the idea of Orientalism as propounded by Edward Said. As a conceptual category, Orientalism is associated with the forms of domination of thought and action, which were established under colonialism. What I am concerned with is not the fixed category of 'The Orient', but the more loosely defined 'east' – loosely defined, because in these centuries, the east was not yet only the countries of Asia. However, by the end of the period under review, the ideas that became part of 'Orientalism' began to be much more clearly defined. What is studied here is thus the travellers' accounts, the continuities visible in accounts across centuries, the clarifications and differences visible in them, and finally, to the extent possible, their impact in their own countries. I must emphasise that the age studied is the pre-modern one, when publication began to be easier, but did not yet cross continental barriers, unlike the travellers themselves. I hope, therefore, that I will succeed in tracing, to some extent, the shift from the broad category of 'east' to the more structured 'Orient'.

This work covers a rather broad span in chronological terms, for I begin with some of the travel writings of the 13th century, and end with some written in the 18th century. Obviously, no attempt can be made to include all the travellers of this period – there are far too many, going in too many different directions, to be able to even mention the majority of the travellers. Any such attempt would end in being a list of names and places, rather than an effort to study their writings and their perceptions. The book is therefore divided

8 Introduction

into six chapters which take us from the imagined to the beginning of colonialism and the 'Orient'. The first chapter is concerned with myths and legends, the second and third go on into the early travels of exploration and the growth of knowledge about the east, while the next three chapters trace the processes by which definitions of the east began to be both more specific and more general – India as rich in produce but with visible poverty, with splendid cities which also had thatched mud houses, which were also, of course, crowded and dirty. The 'orient' was thus beginning to be anchored.

At the same time, the work would be incomplete if I did not at least make the attempt to study the readership of such accounts in their own countries, and, to the extent possible, the way in which these accounts were reflected/located/mentioned in the literature of the country of origin. Here, again, I will not take the entire range, but concentrate, instead, on just the English-language writings, and on the better-known, rather than the more obscure works (better known in the sense of both more recognised, and more easily accessed by a range of readers).

Travel, as exploration and narration of exploration, played the dual role of instructor and storyteller, and in the process, travel narratives began to reconstruct the world through more accurate information. Those who went to these strange lands and returned to tell the story provided knowledge that enabled a shift from the realms of imagination to the regions of reality. Worlds had been, and continued to be, constructed; but now, within these worlds, were clearly defined, named, and delineated regions, which could be rendered on a map, so that others could follow the maps, to arrive at the same places. These worlds thus became more 'fixed', for they were tied down through descriptions of peoples, places, customs, and religions. Knowledge therefore moved from memory, to imagination, from the general to the particular, and then to the familiar and mundane. In the process, the 'east' began to be reconstructed and recast. As knowledge was recast in many forms, the earlier 'exotic' began to lose its lustre, to become ordinary, and often inferior. I must reiterate that this attitude is not to be found in most of the travel accounts used here, but taken out of their time and space, and used in a different set of constructs, they lent themselves to different ways of thinking, understanding, and labelling. It is this that I am most concerned with here. This book is therefore concerned first with some of the travellers – who they were, where they went, and what they wrote. Then, some of the continuities and changes have been traced, before going on to examine, to a rather limited extent, the echoes of travel writing in literature of different kinds.

Notes

1 William Marsden (tr. and ed.), *The Travels of Marco Polo, the Venetian*, London, 1818, revised with an Introduction by John Masefield, London: J.M. Dent and Sons Limited, 1931; New Delhi, Asian Educational Services reprint, 2003, Introduction, p. ix. The five travellers who were taken note of were Herodotus, Gaspar, Melchior, Balthazar and Marco Polo himself.

Introduction 9

2 Guy Miège, *A Relation of Three Embassies from His Sacred Majestie Charles II to the Great Duke of Muscovie, the King of Sweden and the King of Denmark in the Years 1663 & 1664*, London: John Starkey, 1669, https://quod.lib.umich.edu/e/eebo2/A50829.0001.001?view=toc on 20 June 2019, Author's Preface, p. 1.
3 For example, I remember as a child hearing stories from the Mahabharata in a temple. The recitation would often begin by saying "there was a time when Arjuna disturbed Yudhishtira and Draupadi and so had to do penance. On his penance he travelled to . . .". All the places mentioned here were real places which could be located geographically.
4 Mulla Nasruddin was a 13th-century Turkish Sufi, to whom many satirical stories are attributed. Tenali Raman performed a similar role at the court of King Krishnadevaraya of the Vijayanagar Empire at the beginning of the 16th century, while Birbal was a poet at the court of the emperor Akbar in the second half of the same century. All three are remembered for their wisdom, which found expression usually in satirical ways. They can perhaps be compared to the court jesters of European stories. In literature, there is the idea of 'seven major themes' – which argues that any story, written in any time, can be reduced to one or more of those themes. This can be applied to travel stories also. Though they ostensibly fit well with the theme of 'voyage and return', the need for variety makes them move to the other themes – and so, we have fables, science fiction, moral tales, and many more.
5 Romila Thapar, *Sakuntala*, New Delhi: Kali for Women, 2000.
6 We see these in some of the 19th-century writings in India – the 'wily' or 'cunning' or 'crafty' brahmins being among the most common. In other words, these adjectives no longer needed to be used to qualify the caste, for when talking of a brahmin, the adjectival description was taken for granted!
7 Quoted from the *Kitab fi Tahqiq ma lil-Hind* of Abu Raihan Muhammad ibn Ahmad al-Biruni in Muzaffar Alam and Sanjay Subrahmanyam, *Indo-Persian Travels in the Age of Discoveries, 1400–1800*, Cambridge: Cambridge University Press, 2007, p. 1.
8 Edward Farley Oaten, *European Travellers in India During the Fifteenth, Sixteenth and Seventeenth Centuries*, London: Asian Educational Services Reprint, 1909, 1991, pp. 5–7.
9 This can perhaps be seen in the popularity of the books of Bill Bryson and Mark Tully.
10 Benjamin Colber and Glyn Hambrook, "Editors' Introduction", *Comparative Critical Studies*, 4.2, 2007, pp. 165–175, accessed 16 February 2016.
11 Ibid., p. 166.
12 The Baedeker guides were published for a century or more from the 1850s to the 1970s and first in German. It is tempting to argue that this industry was a 19th-century development from the German *Instructions to Travellers* that used to be published in the 15th and 16th centuries.
13 The idea that travel broadens one's horizons remains even in the present-day world as can be seen in the many 'study abroad' programmes that exist in many universities and schools; high school students who have travelled abroad often find that this helps them to get into the colleges of their choice.
14 See, for example, Fred Dallmayr, *Beyond Orientalism: Essays on Cross-Cultural Encounter*, Jaipur: Rawat Publications (reprint), 2001, where he says that South Asia represents a "crossroads of life-forms"; Preface, p. x.
15 Michael Fisher (ed.), *Beyond the Three Seas: Travellers' Tales from Mughal India*, Delhi: Random House India, 2008.
16 Donald F. Lach, *Asia in the Making of Europe*, Vol. 1, Chicago: University of Chicago Press, 1965; Vol. 2, Chicago: University of Chicago Press, 1977; Vol. 3, Chicago: University of Chicago Press, 1993.

10 Introduction

17 See, for example, Paul Starkey and Janet Starkey (eds.), *Travellers in Egypt*, London: Tauris Parke Paperbacks, 2001; David Arnold, *Tropics and the Travelling Gaze: India, Landscape and Science, 1800–1856*, New Delhi: Permanent Black, 2005; Nabil Matar (tr. and ed.), *In the Lands of the Christians: Arabic Travel Writing in the Seventeenth Century*, New York: Routledge, 2003; Michael Fisher (ed.), *Beyond the Three Seas: Travellers' Tales of the Mughal Orient*, Delhi: Random House India, 2007, to mention only a few.
18 Percy G. Adams, *Travelers & Travel Liars 1660–1800*, Berkeley: University of California Press, 1962, p. 1.
19 An Englishman who came to India in the late 16th century and on returning to England provided considerable information about India and her products as well as about Burma and Pegu to the English.
20 Radhika Seshan, "Fabled Lands, Fabulous Wealth: Travel Accounts from the Fourteenth to the Eighteenth Century", presented at the Conference on *On the Road: Writing Travel and Travellers*, Jadavpur University, Kolkata, November 2008.
21 Adams, op.cit., p. 5.
22 The word *safar* means 'journey', and, in Sufi philosophy, it is the term used to describe the journey of life. The philosophy also has mention of halting places en route where one waits for a longer or shorter time until the 'path' ahead is clear once again or at least the direction in which one is to go is identified.

1 The imagined lands

For the ancient European world, the east as seen (or imagined) and defined by Herodotus and the Greeks, was a land of wonder. In the 5th century BCE Herodotus had remarked that "of all the inhabitants of Asia, concerning whom anything is known, the Indians dwell the nearest to the east, and the rising of the sun. Beyond them the whole country is desert on account of the sand."[1] Given that access to this strange land in his time was only through Persia, he naturally attributed the discovery of these eastern lands to Darius, King of the Persians. Darius was amongst the richest of kings because he claimed tribute from India which was paid in gold. This, the earliest 'authority' to speak of India, already gives an indication of the trend of future writings – gold and distance.

Facts and fiction began to be intertwined from this time onwards. So, Herodotus remarked that the Thracians were only slightly less populous than the Indians – an early sign of the size of India's population – and was also the first to talk of cotton. He believed that cotton was an animal fibre, like wool, but later modified the statement to say "wool more beautiful and excellent than the wool of sheep [which] grows on wild trees; these trees supply the Indians with clothing".[2] Interspersed with such statements were some slightly more factual details, as for example about the crocodiles in the Indus river and the speed (and the use) of camels in the desert of India; but a point to be noted is that the two things that constantly struck outside observers, the size of the population and the textiles, can be seen from the earliest mention. Herodotus was the creator (or at least the propagator) of one of the most long-lasting myths about the east, that of the gold-digging ants. "In this desert, there live amid the sand great ants, in size somewhat less than dogs, but bigger than foxes. . . . Those ants make their dwellings under the ground, and like the Greek ants, . . . throw up sand-heaps as they burrow. Now the sand which they throw up is full of gold."[3]

These stories began to be modified slightly after Alexander's conquests, for with the reports that he sent home, knowledge about these distant lands began to be gradually acquired and collated. First of all, these conquests made it clear that neither was India the end of the world, nor was India surrounded by desert. The Greek tradition was of the world being circular,

12   The imagined lands

and so they of course did not believe that beyond India one fell off the end of the world, but India was the 'last outpost of civilisation'. More importantly, though, the conquests opened up a clear and recognisable route to Persia and India, which others could and did follow. Later Greek accounts, like those of Megasthenes, added to the existing information. Texts like the *Milinda Panho* ('The Questions of Menander') make it clear that more accurate information was being sought on a variety of things, for this, as is well known, was an effort at getting more knowledge about the Buddha and Buddhism. Among other things, Alexander's invasion and Megasthenes' account confirmed the size of India's population: thus the Nanda king's army was reported to consist of 100,000 men, probably more than the population of the city of Sparta and about equal to that of the city of Athens. The most important dimension of these reports was to prove that India had a recognisable system of government with kings, ministers, taxes, and justice. These were therefore civilised lands.

From this time onwards, the 'east' basically meant India. Alexander's reports did indicate that India was not the end of the world, but greater knowledge about Asia as a whole had to wait for a few centuries and for the expansion of Roman trade. Roman accounts, particularly Strabo's geography, provided cartographic details about the Indian coastline, but nothing about the interior: and this is despite the volume of Roman trade with India and the information from Roman accounts about the conflict between two rulers of India (the emerging Satavahana power in the Deccan and the Kushanas) over control of the port of Kalyan (near present-day Mumbai). Strabo, following earlier authorities like Megasthenes, pointed out for the first time that no Indian army had ever attacked any outside empire and "nor did any outside army ever invade their country."[4] He also provided additional details about the boundaries of India, as well as an estimate of its size, and clearly pointed to the immensity of the country and its products. He made specific mention of the spices of the south of India. Again following Megasthenes, he remarked on the seven castes into which India's population was divided. Thus, from a fairly early time, the idea of caste was added to the corpus of information about India. However, Strabo scoffed at some of the myths that Megasthenes had propounded, especially about people carrying on wars with cranes and people who slept in their own ears.

But unfortunately, it was these 'fabulous' stories that ended up having a longer lifespan than the more reasoned statements of Strabo. While it took approximately another six centuries before more information about the people of India began to trickle back into Europe, there remained a general and rather hazy knowledge about India, and the trade route across the Indian Ocean was not yet forgotten by European travellers – as can be seen in, for example, the narratives of the two Byzantine writers, the 6th-century CE narratives of Cosmas Indicopleustes about the Malabar Coast, or the early 7th-century CE writings of Theophylact Simocatta. It should be pointed out, here, that such accounts had a rather limited readership, and that they still concentrated on the coast (which of course meant peninsular India), and not the interior. So, while knowledge about the coastline and the ports was still available, nothing was known either about the people further inland from the coast, or about the people of north India. More importantly, there was still a total lack of knowledge about the rest of Asia, including China. Asia still essentially consisted of India, even though Chinese silk had been imported into the Roman Empire, and there was mention of "Seres", the place from which silk came. Theophylact was the first western writer to mention China, about which country he had received information from envoys to the Constantinople court. Once Islam spread across Asia, and as feudalism became more prevalent in Europe, access to, and knowledge of, these distant lands became far less circulated. Distance was both physical and mental, and both were equally difficult to bridge.

In the years after the decline of the Roman Empire, the decline of direct trade to the east and the rise of Islam began to create an increasing physical and mental distance between the 'west' and the 'east'. As the Mediterranean world became more and more part of the Islamic world, relations between the non-Mediterranean countries and the east became steadily more difficult. The old trade networks were taken over mainly by the Arabs, and while the smaller Italian states retained some point of contact, this too was often filtered through the Arab and Turkish networks. Thus, for example, Venetian and Genoese merchants went to Alexandria and Cairo, or overland up to Aleppo but no further.[5] Trade relations between the newly established Islamic states and the Italian republics were resumed after a short break, but this trade was limited, on the European side, to the Mediterranean and Black Sea ports. The horizons of the European world shrank considerably, and when knowledge of other regions existed at all, it was limited and almost invariably 'fantastic' rather than 'factual'. In the medieval world, it was believed that the earth consisted only of the continents of Europe, Asia and Africa, and this belief continued to be held by some people till the 15th century. The Indian Ocean region soon became the unknown and therefore possibly dangerous region.[6]

Notions of difference, which had begun with the stories circulated during the early medieval period, added another layer to the understanding of the east. Early constructions of the east began in the early medieval ages itself when the Roman Empire began to move out of Europe. Byzantium was probably the first 'east'. Over time, differences began to be identified between the Byzantium world and the rest of the former Roman Empire, with the first difference being rooted in religion. The western world came to be called Latin Christendom, while Byzantium was Orthodox.[7] To this early construction was added the fact of the barbarian invasions, affecting the western areas far more than the eastern Empire. The re-conquest of parts of the western Empire under the leadership of Justinian in the 6th century CE, far from re-establishing the Roman Empire, only served to accentuate the changes that had already taken place. His death in 565 CE coincided with the appearance of yet another group of marauders, the Avars, a central Asian group like the Huns. Attacking the Empire from across the Danube, they also managed to get the Slav tribes in the area under their control, and pushed the Lombards, allies of Byzantium, further into Italy.[8] The widening physical and mental gap increased the propensity to define the east as different, therefore mysterious, and often dangerous. Such difference was clear, even in the 'near east', in terms of both religion and language. Both obviously made the mystery greater, and when to the aura of mystery was added lack of knowledge, the east became even farther away.

This kind of nebulous sense of the east being dangerous existed despite the fact that there were still individuals who travelled very comfortably between the western and eastern worlds – for example, Rabbi Benjamin of Tudela in Navarre, who visited Baghdad in the 12th century, and got information about Jews in China and other parts of Asia.[9] But the problem in the western world through this period was that knowledge was restricted to a small group. Even when western scholars began to study Jewish and Arabic writings, they concentrated on physics, astronomy, and medicine, and ignored practical geography. This last had to wait till the Renaissance. Increasingly, barriers of language and culture began to separate not just Muslim and Christian, but also Christians in the east and those in the west. As 'east' and 'west' emerged as different worlds, Byzantium, which straddled both worlds, became perhaps the most problematic.

On the other hand, India, which also lay in the east, seems to have been accepted as different, but not particularly dangerous. India was 'known', in some sense, even if what was known was more fantasy than fact. The only indisputable 'facts' were probably those concerning India's cloth and spices.

The mixture of fact and fantasy that began to colour the ideas of the east naturally gave rise to an amazing number of stories. The east was a great many things to a great many people. So, depending on one's point of view, this was the land where Jesus was born – the Holy Land – or the land of the Saracens (a little later), or the land of milk and honey, for its wealth, or the land of many wonders, not the least of which were its people and products. Given both the lack of knowledge and the consequent myths that emerged about the lands outside the (limited) known world, the number of stories that circulated about the wonders of the east is not surprising. One of the more consistent myths that circulated was that of Prester John.

It is difficult to determine exactly when the legend of Prester John began to circulate in Europe, but it seems to have been widely accepted from about the 12th century. At some time in the middle of the 12th century, a letter began to circulate in Europe, claiming to be from Pester John. There were over 100 different versions of the letter published over the following few centuries. Most often, the letter was addressed to Emanuel I, the Byzantine Emperor of Rome, though other versions were also addressed to the Pope or the King of France. One of the letters said that Prester John's kingdom consisted of seventy-two provinces which included "the Three Indias, and extends to Farther India where the body of St Thomas the Apostle rests. . . . In our territories are found elephants, dromedaries, and camels, and almost every kind of beast that is under heaven."[10] By the 16th century, it was widely accepted that Prester John had written a letter to the Pope, inviting him to depute Christian men to trade in his kingdom.[11]

The 'Three Indias' of the early letters that said that Prester John was the ruler of lands occupied by Christians portrayed a utopian existence, of a kingdom where there was no vice and no crime, despite (or perhaps because of) the abundance of wealth. It was, apparently, the earthly equivalent of the Biblical land of milk and honey, with the added benefit of the Fountain of Youth being located within it, but it was surrounded by barbarians. Prester John therefore wrote the letters to ask for help from other Christians. The letters were taken sufficiently seriously for Pope Alexander III to send someone to search for the land, which was, of course, never found. One problem was that no one knew where to look for it – it was generally believed that the kingdom lay in Asia, but there were also strong supporters for the idea of its being in Africa, in Abyssinia. What no one disputed was that it lay to the east of Europe, for wealth lay in that direction.

More importantly, part of the accumulated knowledge of the east that was still available was of the existence of Christian communities in the east. Thirty years after the preaching of the First Crusade, in 1095, the English historian William of Malmesbury had written

> The world is not evenly divided. Of its three parts, our enemies hold Asia as their hereditary home – a part of the world which our forefathers rightly considered equal to the other two put together. Yet here formerly our Faith put out its branches; here all the Apostles save two met their deaths. But now the Christians of those parts, if there are any left, squeeze a bare subsistence from the soil and pay tribute to their enemies, looking to us with silent longing for the liberty they have lost. Africa, too, the second part of the world, has been held by our enemies by force of arms for 200 years and more, a danger to Christendom all the greater because it formerly sustained the brightest spirits – men whose works will keep the rust of age from Holy Writ as long as the Latin tongue survives. Thirdly, there is Europe, the remaining region of the world. Of this region we Christians inhabit only a part, for who will give the name of Christians to those barbarians who live in the remote islands and seek their living on the icy ocean as if they were whales? This little portion of the world which is ours is pressed upon by warlike Turks and Saracens: for 200 years they have held Spain and the Balearic Islands, and they live in hope of devouring the rest.[12]

The 'known' world had clearly begun to be located in Christianity, while on the outside, but also known, were both the Islamic and the 'other' Christian worlds. Beyond these were the pagan lands; and at this time, the pagans

16 The imagined lands

were possibly better – after all, they did not even profess Christianity, and so had to be totally different, which was perhaps easier to accept than Islam, which had familiar elements and stories, but was still markedly different.

It is difficult to estimate how many travels were undertaken with the aim of finding the kingdom of Prester John, but there is no doubt that it provided ample material for fiction.[13] In Germany, Wolfram von Eschenbach, in *Parsifal*, was the first to unite the legend of the Holy Grail with a history of Prester John; and in English, the author of *The Travels of Sir John Mandeville* went into great detail about the kingdom of Prester John. In the 13th century, Marco Polo identified Prester John with the Khan of the Kereit, a tribe in Mongolia which was then Nestorian Christian. Others continued searching for him in China. In the 15th century the Portuguese looked for Prester John all over Africa, and especially in Ethiopia, while others were sure that the legendary king lived in Kerala, India. In the middle of the 16th century, the King of Ethiopia was nicknamed 'Prester John' by the Europeans, and it has been said that the description of the search for Prester John reads like a detective story.[14]

Among the many works that talk of the land of Prester John, and achieved a remarkable level of longevity and reading, was *The Travels of Sir John Mandeville*. It was first published in 1499 by Wrykyn de Worde. Purporting to be a travelogue, it described the journey of a nobleman, Sir John Mandeville. He had killed his opponent in a duel, and as penance was instructed by the King to leave England and travel to Jerusalem. He dutifully left England in 1322 to make his way across the known world. The book acquired considerable popularity in its own time and later, and was one of the accounts used by Columbus to justify his search for the route across the Atlantic Ocean. In 1725, a freshly edited version was published, and school stories published for the English reading public in the early decades of the 20th century mentioned the travel as 'suitable reading' for school children.[15] The wider English-reading public, brought up on a diet of John Mandeville, was probably rather horrified when it was discovered that the entire book was an artful putting together of many stories and some accounts of earlier travellers, particularly Friar Odoric, and there was no such person as Sir John Mandeville who travelled across Europe and part of Asia.

As mentioned earlier, *Mandeville* was believed to be a genuine travelogue and was therefore influential in the multiple constructions of the east. Its authenticity was in considerable degree established through the early sections of the book, where the way to Jerusalem and the Holy Lands was described. These routes had already been well established thanks to the Crusades and the later pilgrimages, and as the book reiterated existing belief, there was no reason to doubt the existence of the traveller – one more among the many that travelled across Europe to Jerusalem. Everyone also knew that beyond Jerusalem lay the fabulous lands of Asia; and so, when the travelogue moved into descriptions of Asia, a shift into the realms of fantasy was possibly both expected and accepted. The way to Asia was long and complicated, and so, said Mandeville, it was better for the traveller to go first to the land of Prester John. As stories of Prester John were already current, and there was a vague association of the east with Prester John, and as India was the only east that was known, Prester John had to be the ruler of India. Mandeville therefore calls him the 'Emperor of Ind', king of a large kingdom which had many "full noble cities and good towns" and "many great diverse isles and large".[16] However, by this time Marco Polo's account was also beginning to be known, and therefore there was some knowledge about the wealth of China. According to Mandeville, despite the existence of so many cities and islands, Prester John's land was not as rich as that of "the great Chan" for it was "too far to travel to". This meant that, even though goods were cheaper in his land, merchants feared "the long way and the great perils in the sea in those parts."[17] There is a long description about a valley that had to be traversed before getting to the land of Prester John and this valley was called "Vale Perilous". This was always "full of devils and hath been always".[18] This valley could be crossed only by "good Christian men, that be stable in the faith".[19] Considerable detail was provided about how the name 'Prester' came to be assigned to a king in preference to the more common title of 'king', as well as about the different kinds of people in the empire.[20]

These were truly the fabulous lands. The travels provide no geographical identification for India or the land of Prester John. That India existed was known, partly through the produce of India, partly through the reports of the Crusaders on the products from India that were available in the Holy Lands, and probably much more through the continued circulation of the stories of Alexander having conquered Asia up to India. Fabulous lands had to have fabulous people – thus Mandeville talks of an 'isle', "where the folk be great giants of twenty-eight foot long or of thirty foot long",[21] and other islands which had "full cruel and full evil women of nature [who had] precious stones in their eyes".[22] Older information about crocodiles which had been in Herodotus now began to be re-circulated along with stories about serpents and sea monsters.[23] Mandeville's account fed into these fables when he talked of India having strange animals and birds – "cockodrills", "orafles", and "gerfaunts".[24] All that is missing, in fact, is the story of the gold-digging ants!

Much more impressive than the natural wonders was the immense wealth, also something to be marvelled at. In 14th-century Europe, gold and silver plates were used only by the upper nobility, and even they usually dined off plain wooden tables. Vessels were pewter, copper or iron; but Prester John's land had vessels made of precious stones, and tables also made of similar precious material (particularly emerald and amethyst). Population was also much larger than in the known world, so that when Prester John went to war he carried with him "three great crosses" and for the protection of these crosses alone, and not as part of the general army, there were 100,000 men. Constantly underpinning the entire narrative are more accurate statements, such as, for example, that the routes to India were known to the Venetian

18   *The imagined lands*

and Genoese merchants (Indian produce was disseminated throughout Europe mainly from these places).

Mandeville then moved on to a description of India. The land of the 'Indies' was described as being of "full many diverse countries". It was called 'Ind' after a "flom that runneth throughout the country. . . . In that flom men find eels of thirty foot long and more. And the folk that dwell nigh that water be of evil colour, green and yellow."[25] This perhaps harks back to the stories of the Indus, and the crocodiles in that river. In and around India were "more than 5000 isles", almost all of which were densely populated, and had large numbers of cities. One of these 5,000 was the isle of Chana, the ruler of which was "wont to be so strong and so mighty that he held war against King Alexander."[26]

It is statements such as these that made the *Travels* more 'real', for there was a very careful weaving together of what was known, what was speculation, and what was fantasy. The story of Alexander's war against Porus, on the bank of the Chenab, was familiar to many western readers, for Alexander's exploits were fairly well known, as was the fact that he had turned back from the conquest of India. Equally well known was the virtual monopoly that Venetian and Genoese merchants had over Asiatic produce, and the merchandise was both highly priced and highly prized. The land from which this wealth came had to be fabulous. This was a story which was firmly believed in by almost all Europeans even till the mid-17th century.

All of Asia, not just Prester John's land, was immensely wealthy. Proof, in *Mandeville*, is provided by the references to diamonds and pearls. There existed in Europe at the time a certain amount of knowledge of both these gems; so, while it was known that pearls came from the sea, there was no such clear knowledge of where exactly diamonds were to be found. We have in *Mandeville* a very interesting passage about diamonds growing on crystal rocks, and there being male and female diamonds, which were nourished by 'the dew of heaven' to become naturally square – just as pearls were by nature round. He then went into the way in which pepper grew on trees in one of the isles of the Indies. Beyond the Indies lay Cathay – China – a land of silk, Mongols, and many other 'curiosities'. However, the Mongols also made it a land to be wary of, unlike India, from where no marauders had swept the known universe.

Mandeville's Indies are indeed a fabulous land, and I am using the word 'fabulous' here both in the material sense of fabulous wealth, and in the imaginative sense of the land of fables. The fact was that these lands provided goods not available in Europe, but which Europe needed. Lacking knowledge of the actual areas of production, an imaginary world was created, one which suited the luxury and, again, 'fabulous' materials that came from there. The creator of Mandeville also put all his stories into a believable knowledge structure – thus, he talked (pseudo-learnedly) of the Septentrion (the northern regions), the tropics, and went into supposedly learned details of latitudes. All this fit into the existing state of knowledge of the 14th century, without adding in any substantial way to that knowledge.

The Travels of Sir John Mandeville, accepted as genuine, became part of the general reading of Europe. Even when more accurate information began to be available, *Mandeville* remained popular, perhaps because the work was so easy and interesting to read, in contrast to the more 'erudite' and factual works that began to make their appearance. Some of the more exaggerated statements, in slightly later centuries, could be dismissed in a fashion similar to the way in which, in modern times, the 'fishermen's tales' are dismissed – with the assumption of a kernel of truth.

Another dimension of myths and myth making was cartography. Medieval and Renaissance maps often included images of a wide variety of mythical sea monsters and occasionally monsters on land as well. Chet Van Duzer has shown that Nicholas of Cusa, a 15th-century "philosopher, theologian and astronomer, drew a comparison between the cartographer and God: as God created the world, the cartographer creates an image of the world."[27] As part of what he calls the 'geography of the marvellous', these maps were of crucial importance in both the myth making, and in the process of explaining the exotic other. It is noticeable that, even in the early 17th century, in travel accounts such as those of Thomas Herbert,[28] there is at least one reference to sharks, and to sharks attacking the ships. The sharp dorsal fin of the shark in reality is also reminiscent of the earlier imaginaire of *serra*, the sawfish which was reputed to live off the coast of Africa, both the Atlantic and the Indian Ocean sides, and attack the wooden ships of the Indian sailors. The Catalan atlas of 1375 shows sirens in the Indian Ocean, and Marco Polo declared that the pearl divers on the eastern coast of India used charms to keep away sea monsters when they were under water. Of course, they themselves could not cast the charms, and so paid others, presumably brahmins, to "pay those men who charm the great fishes."[29]

These stories continued to remain in circulation and are even today seen in the stories of Sindbad the Sailor. The great roc, the regular shipwrecks, and all of Sindbad's fantastic adventures, which always ended in him returning safe home, are perhaps the template for some of the travel accounts of these centuries. The land beyond the sea, and the life in the sea as well as on the other side of the sea, remained fascinating, and can be seen in fiction as disparate as Jonathan Swift's *Gulliver's Travels*, Daniel Defoe's *Robinson Crusoe*, R.L. Stevenson's *Treasure Island*, and Rudyard Kipling's short story, *The White Seal*.

Prester John, the fabulous lands of the east, and perhaps the desire to actually face the sea monsters and to either prove they existed or come back with a factual account, all played into both the imagination of the east and the search for the true east. Locating these lands in reality and explaining that reality to a European audience thus became the cornerstone of travelling to the fabulous east.

20 *The imagined lands*

Notes

1. George Rawlinson (tr. and ed.), *Herodotus Histories*, Wordsworth Editions of World Literature, 1996.
2. Ibid., p. 271.
3. Ibid., p. 270.
4. Strabo, *Book XV*, On India, internet archive, www.und.ac.za/und/classics/india/strabo.htm, accessed 14 March 2012.
5. It is interesting to speculate that this was because beyond these places lived the strange world of Islam and the stranger world of different denominations of Christians. But this remains a speculation.
6. This can be best seen in the medieval maps, where the edges of the earth were depicted with fantastic and mythical creatures, and the words "Here be danger." This can be seen in the *Carta Marina*, https://upload.wikimedia.org/wikipedia/commons/e/e5/Carta_Marina_AB_stitched.jpg, accessed 21 June 2019.
7. To misquote Bernard Shaw, "these were two countries divided by a common belief." (The original quotation is supposed to be "two countries divided by a common language", but the attribution has been questioned, for the sentence is not found in his published work).
8. I have written about this in greater detail in Radhika Seshan, "Identity Formation, Foundational Myths and Communalism: Western Europe and India", published in *The ICFAI Journal of History and Culture*, 1.1, May 2007, pp. 56–72.
9. Ronald Latham (tr. and ed.), *Marco Polo: The Travels*, Penguin Books, 1958, Introduction, p. 8.
10. Edward Brooke-Hitching, *The Phantom Atlas: The Greatest Myths, Lies and Blunders on Maps*, London: Simon & Schuster, 2016, p. 195.
11. Edward Ullendorff and Charles Fraser Beckingham, *The Hebrew Letters of Prester John*, Oxford: Oxford University Press, 1982. There are believed to be some 100 manuscripts in libraries across Europe that deal with the myth, with the Hebrew letters being only one of the languages in which the manuscripts are written. See also Rila Mukherjee, "The Strange History of Prester John across the Indian Ocean", *Asian Review of World History*, 6.2, 2018.
12. Richard William Southern, *The Making of the Middle Ages*, Yale: Yale University Press, 1961, p. 71.
13. Even in the 1950s *Prester John* was a detective story that was supposed to be read by English school children.
14. E. Denison Ross, "Prester John and the Empire of Ethiopia", Arthur P. Newton (ed.), *Travel and Travellers of the Middle Ages*, New York: Barnes & Noble, 1968 (first published in 1926), pp. 174–194; C.F. Beckingham, "The Quest for Prester John", *Bulletin of the John Rylands University Library*, 62, 1980, pp. 290–310.
15. See for example, Elinor M. Brent-Dyer's *Chalet School* Series published from 1929 onwards. There references are to be found in the early books and not in the later books of the series.
16. Sir Alfred William Pollard (ed.), *The Travels of Sir John Mandeville, with Three Narratives in Illustration of It: The Voyage of Johannes de Plano Carpini, the Journal of William de Rubruquis, and the Journal of Friar Odoric from Hakluyt's "Navigations, Voyages and Discoveries"*, London: Macmillan & Co, 1900, p. 178.
17. Ibid.
18. Ibid., p. 185.
19. Ibid., p. 186.
20. See Radhika Seshan, "From Mandeville to Mundy: Sources for the Study of Medieval India", Radhika Seshan (ed.), *Convergences: Rethinking India's Past*,

New Delhi: Primus Books, 2014, pp. 55–62, for a brief discussion on a possible connection between John Bunyan's *The Pilgrim's Progression* and Mandeville's discussion of the way to the land of Prester John.
21 Ibid., p. 187.
22 Ibid., p. 188. It's interesting that 'evil women of nature' possibly worked here like an oxymoron.
23 As an aside, we could perhaps point to a fairly famous Mughal painting of Akbar's time by Miskin which has dragons, serpents, and crocodiles together with more familiar animals and birds.
24 Mandeville, op.cit., p. 188.
25 Ibid., p. 108.
26 Ibid., p. 110.
27 Chet Van Duzer, *Sea Monsters on Medieval and Renaissance Maps*, London: The British Library, 2014, p. 11.
28 Thomas Herbert, *Some Years Travels into Africa and Asia the Great, Especially Describing the Famous Empires of Persia and Industant: As also Divers Other Kingdoms in the Orientall Indies, and Iles Adjacent*, London: Jacob Blome and Richard Bishop, 1638, accessed through Google Books, January 2011. See particularly p. 7 showing a shark with a human in its mouth. This image may also go back to the Biblical story of Jonah being thrown overboard to a sea monster so that the ship that he was on would be saved. See also Peter Mundy, *The Travels of Peter Mundy, in Europe and Asia, 1608–1667*, Vol. 2: *Travels in Asia, 1628–1634*, London: Hakluyt Society, 1914, facing p. 16, showing a shark as well as the capture of a shark using a chain and a hook. Compare this with the image in Chet Van Duzer, ibid., p. 51.
29 Henry Yule (tr. and ed.), *The Book of Ser Marco Polo, the Venetian*, London: J. Murray, 1903, Chapter 16. See Chet Van Duzer, ibid., Fig. 27, p. 46 for the visual representation of pearl divers with fish moving away from them.

2 Locating the east

> And as regards this India I have inquired from many who have knowledge of the matter, and they all assured me as with one voice that it includeth in its limits a good twenty-four thousand islands, in which there are sixty-four crowned kings.
>
> For in the whole world there be no such marvels as in that realm of India.
> – Friar Odoric of Pordenone[1]

The European world once again came more into general contact with the lands to the east only after the end of the 11th century and the preaching of the Crusades. The desire to serve Christianity, the increasing emphasis on display of piety through pilgrimage, and perhaps just the wish to visit and explore lands other than one's own all led to a revival of interest in travel. More accurate knowledge and texts about the east were the logical corollary. One century later came the next shock from the east – the Mongol raids.

This 'holocaust out of the east' undoubtedly horrified the western world, but maybe, in some ways, also gratified them. The medieval Islamic world, in particular, had been no stranger to the warlike tribes of Central Asia, but the Mongols were probably something new even in their experience. The united tribes of the Mongols, under the leadership of Changez Khan, swept out of Mongolia in 1206, and, in short order, established an empire, the size of which was unmatched then or later. In Asia, perhaps the only large country left unconquered was India.

The Mongol attacks only reinforced a perception that had begun as early as Roman times, when the east had begun to be seen as dangerous. From here had come in succession raids by the Wends, the Magyars and later the Huns. The Huns had appeared in Europe in the 4th century and attacks by other barbarians had followed. Until the Mongol attacks, the Huns had probably set the standard in ferocity. None of the experiences of attacks from the east had, however, prepared the European world for the Mongols, for the scale and the ferocity of the Mongols were outside their experience. The techniques of warfare, speed of attack, the range of distances and the time taken to traverse them, the ability to travel without pack animals, and the Mongol method of fighting on and from horseback were all unknown to the Europeans.

Levels of curiosity and fear and fascination with and about these new creatures was obviously immense. The entry of the Mongols proved something that had been long known – that there were unknown but inhabited lands beyond the boundaries of the familiar world. India of course lay somewhere in these lands, but there were others, about which knowledge was required. Moving away from the Roman 'Seres', as well as the general statements about the world consisting of three parts, there was now a desire to know more about both the other parts – Africa and Asia. The emphasis was on Asia as the land of both curiosities and dangers. Knowledge of this world would perhaps lead to better methods of combating, accommodating, or getting profit from the inhabitants of these lands. This meant, naturally, that the acquisition of first-hand knowledge, to the extent possible, was urgent. And as the Crusades had taken Europeans into the 'near' east, so also the influx from further east demanded that travellers go further in search of the lands from which these dangers had come.

The Christian world actually suffered far less than the Islamic one as a result of the Mongol incursions, even though, to the Christians, it seemed as if they were the hordes of Satan, out to overrun and destroy their world. In 1260, an appeal for unity was issued by the then Pope, Alexander IV, declaring that in the face of the impending "wars of universal destruction" it was the duty of all good Christians to "take provident action against a peril impending and palpably approaching".[2] Nevertheless, there seemed to be at least a faint silver lining in that, as these Mongols were still 'heathens', they could perhaps be converted to Christianity, and their aid then enlisted against Islam. Thus, in the 13th century, proselytising and diplomatic missions began. Three friars were among the earliest to go into these lands – Johannes de Plano Carpini (sent by Pope Innocent IV) in 1245, William de Rubruquis (sent by the King of France) in 1253, and, a little later, Odoric of Pordenone (in 1330). As the first to travel into Mongol country, they provided first-hand information about both the Mongols and the lands they inhabited. This included information about the lands of Asia other than India, and so the accounts of the Friars are very important in understanding the ways in which the 'east' began to be constructed.

Carpini, the first of these travellers, had, as mentioned earlier, been appointed by Pope Innocent IV to travel into Mongol lands in order to, first, get information, and, second, possibly convert them to Christianity. He returned to Lyons in 1247 and then wrote what is one of the most famous pieces of medieval travel literature, the *History of the Mongols*. He travelled through Bohemia and Poland, then to the Russian city of Kiev, after which he entered Mongol-held lands. He went down the Dnieper River to the Black Sea and then made his way to the camp of Batu Khan (Changez Khan's grandson). Leaving this camp, he travelled further across the Volga basin and then into Mongolia proper along what was apparently a well-travelled route, for he says that "we spared no horse-flesh, but rode swiftly and without intermission, as fast as our horses could trot." He reached Karakorum in July 1246 in time to witness the coronation of the new Khan at the end of August 1246. He was given permission to leave in September 1246, but finally left only in November, to reach Kiev in June 1247, and Lyons at the end of the year. His writing can perhaps be said to indicate the trend of future travel literature and accurate information, for he gave details about direction (where the lands lay in relation to Europe), the people, and some of the customs. He said that the country of the Mongols lay "in that part of the world which is thought to be most north easterly. . . . In some part thereof it is full of mountains, and in other places plain and smooth ground, but everywhere sandy and barren, neither is the hundredth part thereof fruitful. . . . Whereupon they have neither villages, nor cities among them, except one called Cracurim [Karakorum], and is said to be a proper town."[3]

Perhaps most surprising to him was not the coronation itself but the magnificence of the ceremony and the number of people who attended, who included "Duke Jeroslav of Susdal in Russia, and a great many dukes of the Cathayans and of the Solangi".[4] Other delegates included the two sons of the King of Georgia, a representative of the Caliph of Baghdad and more than ten "sultans of the Saracens". In the time that he spent at Karakorum, Carpini acquired as much information as possible on the Mongols and their customs. He said that there were many things that he observed among the Mongols that were worthy of praise. Carpini pointed in particular to the tradition of obedience among them, saying that they were

> more obedient unto their lords and masters, than any other either clergy or lay-people in the whole world. . . . They seldom or never fall out among themselves, and as for fightings or brawlings, wounds or manslaughters, they never happen among them. There are neither thieves nor robbers of great riches to be found, and therefore the tabernacles and carts of them that have any treasures are not strengthened with locks or bars. . . . Their women are chaste, neither is there so much as a word uttered concerning their dishonesty.[5]

However, the fabulous was not missing in his accounts. Thus, there were creatures in the deserts near Armenia who

> had each of them but one arm and one hand growing out of the midst of their breast, and but one foot. Two of them used to shoot in one bow, and they ran so swiftly that horses could not overtake them. They ran also upon that one foot by hopping and leaping, and being weary of such walking, they went upon their hand and their foot, turning themselves round, as it were in a circle.[6]

Other sights included

> the Parossitae, people of the Arctic, who having little stomachs and small mouths, eat not anything at all, but seething flesh they stand or sit over the pot, and receiving the steam or smoke thereof, are therewith only nourished, and if they eat anything it is very little.[7]

Carpini also repeated the stories of the dog-headed men who spoke in a mixture of speech and barks. The east, in other words, continued to be populated by strange creatures. The Mongols were in comparison perhaps rather better, for however ferocious and bloodthirsty, they were still human. They did look different from "all other people", because they were "broader between the eyes, and the balls of their cheeks, than men of other nations".[8]

Rubruquis was the next of the travellers, sent by the French king in 1253. He too got as far as Karakorum, but apparently followed a slightly different route to get there, for he went from France to the Black Sea and then overland. His was, however, probably the more familiar route, for he took the well-established Crusader and pilgrimage route up to Acre. Like Carpini, he was also on an information-gathering mission, and so, like his predecessor, he also commented on all that the Mongol lands had or did not have. Again, like his predecessor, he too found that the most noticeable difference was the lack of cities; "in no place any settled city to abide in, neither know they of the celestial city to come."[9] Here was an early construction of the east, distinct from both the west and from India. City life was familiar to western Europeans of the 13th century, and there was a definite appreciation of the wealth of the city-states and mercantile republics of Italy. And that India had (and had always had) a large number of cities, was well-known enough to be almost a cliché.[10] But here was a huge population which apparently did not live within the recognised confines of a city. And so, particularly strange to these travellers was the nomadic lifestyle, where a camp looking like a 'great village' could be established and struck within a few hours. But, as said earlier, these strange people were still human, and as humans, surely had some traits that were familiar. Therefore, the familiar needed to be identified. Such identifiable, though still distinct features could be found in geography, social practices, or community life. For Rubruquis it lay in the second. He pointed to the practice among the Mongols of delivering a certain amount of produce to the lord's house every third day, and this he compared to Syria, where one third of the produce of every serf was given to the lord.[11] Additional familiarity lay in the presence of a recognisable hierarchy of the lord and those who obeyed him.

Unlike Carpini, Rubruquis was not particularly impressed by anything in the Mongol lands, least of all the cities of tents. He appreciated the speed with which they could be set up and dismantled, but they obviously did not compare with a properly constructed city. The only city was Karakorum, which also was not that large, for he said that "exclusive of the palace of the khan, it was not as big as [the Parisian suburb of] St. Denis, and the monastery of St. Denis is ten times larger than the palace."[12] On the other hand, St. Denis probably did not have the number of people from different countries who were present there:

> ambassadors from Byzantium and Baghdad, from the King of Delhi, from the Seljuks of Asia Minor, from emirs of Syria and Iraq, from princes of Russia. There was even a colony of European residents who apparently had been brought back as captives during the Mongol raids of the previous decade: a goldsmith from Paris who had a Hungarian wife, an Alsatian woman married to a Russian architect, and a certain Basil, the son an Englishman, who was born in Hungary.[13]

It was this variety of people that was impressive; for here was a cross sample of the entire Mongol empire, and of those who needed to negotiate or just be visible in that Empire's spheres of activity.

He was also not very comfortable with the Mongol bands that he met on the roads, for he declared that each band needed to be paid before the travellers could proceed further. In fact, the first Mongols they met, he said,

> began impudently to beg our victuals from us. And we gave them some of our biscuit and wine, which we had brought with us from the town of Soldia. And having drunk off one flagon of our wine they demanded another, saying that a man goeth not into the house with one foot.[14]

His writing seems to imply that the Mongol demands were understandable because the Mongols were, after all, heathens and pagans. However, his greatest animosity was reserved for the Nestorians whom he met at Karakorum, regarding them as poor excuses for Christians. He was also rather unhappy to find Muslims at the courts of the different Khans, given that he had been sent there in the hope of getting the Mongols to convert to Christianity. The obviously well-established Muslim presence probably seemed to him to signal an end to those hopes even before they could even be enunciated.

Both these were 13th-century travellers who were, for the first time, exposed to a way of life totally different from that with which they were familiar. Thus (as with all travellers), they looked for the familiar in an unfamiliar world, and pointed to that which was totally strange. Both knew that there were Christians in the lands controlled by the Mongols, but the tone of the writings shows a greater distrust of these Christians, mainly Nestorians, than of the Mongols – the Nestorian practices were known and criticised, Mongol practices were unknown. Proselytising activities were necessary also to make sure that these 'heathens' were not converted to the Nestorian belief. The Mongols were known to be the most fearsome fighters the world had until then known. Not surprisingly, the travellers were both curious and wary of these unknown people. On the one hand, therefore, while both praised the Mongols' traits of loyalty and obedience, both were also quick to point out that this obedience, or any other positive quality, was limited to their own people. Both Carpini and Rubruquis said that they were insolent and hostile to strangers, and that it was not counted a crime among them to steal from or attack those not of their own tribe or family.

Clear in these works is the awe of the military ability of the Mongols. Carpini, in particular, went into great detail about the methods to be followed by the European soldiers who had to face them. Technologically, the Mongols may (or may not) have been more advanced. They were definitely better trained, and were able to make better use of the tools that they did have. Their way of sharpening arrows, by dipping the arrowheads while red hot into boiling salt water, was recommended as a method that the Europeans should adopt. The Friars also displayed a not very grudging respect for the tactics used by the Mongols in battle. For example, soldiers and commanders were advised not to pursue fleeing (or supposedly fleeing) Mongol soldiers, as this was often a deliberate strategy used for ambush.[15]

These accounts do not show any traces of any feeling of superiority. Difference was both expected and accepted. Rubruquis, for instance, stated that, when leaving Constantinople, he felt that he had entered a "different world".[16] If differences were accepted, the basis for difference had to be made explicit, and so we have in both the accounts a great many details about the way the Mongols lived, about their customs, their houses, and their wealth. Perhaps the most surprising aspect of the Mongol establishments to these travellers was that, though nomadic, they were wealthy, and in an identifiable fashion.

Both travellers talked about the wealth of the tribes and made it clear that this wealth consisted of the more recognisable forms of wealth – gold, silver, silk, etc. – as well as cattle and horses. Carpini said that they had "more horses and mares than all the world", as well as camels, oxen, sheep, and goats.[17] Rubruquis, while talking of the staple drink of the Mongols, something he called 'cosmos' or mares' milk, said that the Duke of the region was supplied with the milk of 3,000 mares.[18] Rubruquis further said that the Duke had "thirty cottages or granges" near his own camp, but neither of them talked about ownership of land. Presumably, the Mongols did not have a system of private property that could be clearly identified as such by the Europeans. In the middle of all this, it was probably something of a relief for them that the more familiar forms of wealth (i.e. gold, silver, etc.) were, as in Europe, limited to the upper classes.

One point to be noted about both these travellers is that they did not actually get to China proper, only to Mongolia. The Mongol empire, after the death of Changez Khan, had been divided into three main sections, each under one Mongol Khan. The Khanate of the west corresponded roughly to European Russia, the Khanate of the Levant stretched from Eastern Persia to the Mediterranean Sea, and the Khanate of Central Asia consisted of the Transoxiana region. Both Carpini and Rubruquis seem to have travelled across all three, but finally stayed for any length of time only at Karakorum. Their knowledge of the Mongols was derived from the travel itself, and from what they observed at Karakorum. The different world, for them, thus began from across the Danube itself, and once they crossed the Volga, they were in altogether strange lands. This was *their* east – different from the 'near' east, which consisted mainly of the lands on the eastern Mediterranean seaboard; and, perhaps harking back to the Roman Empire, when barbarians lived to the north and the east, here too were barbaric lands. 'Barbarian' from Roman times had been virtually synonymous with uncivilised, but it is noticeable that neither of these travellers refer to the Mongols as either barbaric or uncivilised. 'Different', as said earlier, was not (yet) seen as necessarily inferior or uncivilised. On the other hand, included in the 'different', from as early as the 9th century, was Byzantium – so the idea of Byzantium as 'east' was to some extent reinforced by their writings.

Friar Odoric of Pordenone was the next traveller into the lands of the Mongols, and unlike the earlier friars, he did travel to India and further east. It is with him that we start getting more detailed accounts of the wealth of Asia. Beginning at Venice, and crossing over the "greater sea", he made his way to Trebizond, which he said was "a haven for the Persians, Medes and all the people on the further side of the sea".[19] On reaching Persia, he went first to the city of

> Tauris . . ., which was in old time called Susis. This is a nobler city for merchandise than any other which at this day existeth in the world . . . and the Christians will tell you that the emperor there hath more revenue from that one city than the king of France hath from his whole realm.[20]

From this city he travelled eastwards in a caravan and reported that he had stopped for a few days at Kashan (halfway between Isfahan and Tehran), which he said had been "greatly destroyed" by the Tartars. The next city he went to was Yazd, which he declared to be "the third best city" in Persia, but in which, according to the Saracens, "no Christian is ever able to live . . . beyond one year."[21] Odoric provides no explanation for this statement. All these were part of what he called Chaldaea.

For Odoric, trained in the biblical tradition, Chaldaea was the much more familiar name, but was practically indistinguishable from Persia itself. For him, the difference between the two lay apparently not so much in location, but in language and people. He said the Chaldaeans had a language of their own, which he apparently did not understand; but what he remarked on particularly was that "the men are comely, but the women in sooth of an ill favour." The men, he declared, were smartly dressed and wore jewels, but the women had "nothing on them but a miserable shift reaching to their knees ... and their hair neither plaited nor braided". From Chaldaea he travelled to "inland India".[22]

It is noticeable that, for Odoric, India was the point of reference, and so travel to India involved moving through different lands. For him, these lands were parts of India itself. 'Inland India' was the region near the Persian Gulf, while 'Upper India' was China. When he referred to China in any other words (which was rare), it was as Cathay or as the land of the Great Khan. It was from inland India that he could come to India proper through the city of Ormuz, "a city strongly fenced and abounding in costly wares". However, it was not a healthy place to live in for it was too hot and there were no trees or fresh water. Unlike earlier travellers, who merely commented on the places they saw and on the people who lived there, Odoric had begun to move to the idea of outsiders living in these lands, and, at least as an undercurrent, the differences between the people of east and west were also beginning to be highlighted. While difference had always existed, now writing was beginning to make these differences clearer.

With the entry into India, Odoric's narrative seems to shift to more detailed descriptions, both of territory and the material aspects. He was among the first to say that there was a distinctive ship that sailed in this region that was built without any iron. Landing at a port that he called 'Tana', possibly the port of Thatta in Sind, or the old port of Thana, now a part of Mumbai (Bombay) and not the port of Tana on the Black Sea, he went on to describe it as the area in which Alexander had fought a major battle with Porus.[23] As said earlier, the Alexander stories were apparently familiar in the western world, whether or not they were current in India at that time.

His account gives a number of descriptions of things that he found strange. Of particular interest to him were first the animals, and then the customs of the people. He described the black lions to be seen near the port, and the baboons and bats ('as big as pigeons'). He also remarked on the size of the rats, and said that as cats were of no use in catching them, the people used dogs. Women, he said, went about naked, and at the time of a girl's marriage, she was "set on a horse, and the husband gets on the crupper and holds a knife pointed at her throat" – an interesting variation, it seems, on the later idea of marriage at gunpoint!

As with the earlier Friars, there was an attempt to explain the unfamiliar in relation to that which was familiar – so for example, he said that in the "kingdom of Mobar"[24] there was an idol as

> big as St. Christopher commonly represented by the painters, and it is entirely of gold, seated on a great throne, which is also of gold. And round its neck it hath a collar of gems of immense value. And the church of this idol is also of pure gold, roof (and walls) and pavement.[25]

What made the Friar's account particularly valuable was his description of pepper production. He went into considerable detail about the 'pepper forest', and about the pepper that grew on the vine in a fashion similar to grapes in Europe, and, again like grapes, were gathered when they were ripe. The exotic and the different were once again juxtaposed here, for along with the description of the forest, he named the cities on either side, and then mentioned that the rivers were full of "evil crocodiles i.e. serpents . . . and a variety of beasts which are not found in our Frank countries."[26] He was possibly the first European traveller to describe the practice of sati, which he described as a "detestable custom", and remarked that while the law was that the wife should be burnt with her husband, the reverse did not apply, so that he could then remarry.

There were other stories which also emphasised the differences visible in the east. For instance, when he talked of Sumatra, his descriptions included women and the customs. Thus, he said that "in that country all the women be in common; and no one there can say, this is my wife or this is my husband" – something very strange to him, obviously. He went on to comment on the prevalence of cannibalism, and the fact that houses were seen as private property. (Can one also perhaps postulate that this was yet another marker of difference – that houses were clearly property, but women were 'common to all'?) He said that Java was "the second best of all islands that exist",[27] which had all kinds of spices "and great abundance of all victuals except wine". The king of the island had a "sumptuous palace", the largest he had ever seen, in which one staircase was of silver, another of gold, and the walls were covered with beaten gold, on which were engraved pictures decorated with precious stones.[28]

Fitting in with the existing state of knowledge of geography at the time, where beyond the known lands lay the edge of the world, he said that beyond Java, to the south, lay the "Dead Sea, the water whereof runneth ever towards the south. . . . And if the shipmen go but a little way from the shore they are carried rapidly downwards and never return again."[29]

From Java, Odoric went on to another country which he called Campa (Champa) of which the strangest feature was that "several kind of fishes in those seas come swimming towards the country in such abundance, that, for a great distance into the sea, nothing can be seen but the backs of fishes."[30] It is tempting to speculate that this fed into the idea that was enunciated later, in the 19th century in particular, that Asians did not have to work as hard as the Europeans to earn their living, and so were 'naturally' lazy – for if fish came swimming in, there was naturally no need to make any special effort to catch them!

Travelling on into China, where he stayed for three years, he had the opportunity to observe the administration at close quarters. He described it as being "by governors of tens, governors of hundreds, and governors of thousands," and was thus most efficient. Here too he went into details of the wealth, not just of the king but also of the lords – at a banquet, each of 14,000 lords wore "a garment of gold and precious stones, which is worth ten thousand florins."[31] The city of Canton was said to be "as big as three

Locating the east 31

Venices", with more craft in that one city than the whole of Italy, and with so much shipping that it was beyond description. Points of comparison were constantly provided, so that his readers could use their imagination to good effect when reading his account – even if the account was meant only for Church readership.

In some ways, Odoric was echoing possibly the most famous of all travel accounts, that of Marco Polo, which acquired immense popularity in its own time and later. Marco and his bothers Maffeo and Nicolo began their travels into the eastern lands by accident but continued by design. In 1250 they left Venice and went to Constantinople and there they decided that better profit would be had by going into the Black Sea area. Reaching the port of Soldaia on that sea, they then travelled inland and reached the court of "a powerful chief of the Western Tartars, named Barka, who . . . had the reputation of being one of the most liberal and civilised princes hitherto known amongst the tribes of Tartary." For the first time, therefore, they provided an alternative view of the Mongols which described them within structures more known to the western world – courts, money, and trade. They stayed for a year at Barka's court but just as they decided to leave and go back to Constantinople, war broke out. Unable to travel westwards, they travelled east to Bokhara and there met an ambassador from Kublai Khan's court. This ambassador invited them to travel with him into the further eastern lands and go to Kublai Khan's court in China.

Marco described the overland route traversing Armenia, what he called Turkomenia, into Persia, further overland into Mongolia and into China. On the way he did take the occasional detour (both real and literary); and therefore, when talking of Persia, described the manufactures of Baghdad, the route from Baghdad to Basra, and stated that Basra lay at the head of the Persian Gulf which was 'commonly called the Sea of India'. These lands were still 'India', so there were three Indias – the Greater, the Lesser, and the Middle. Greater India was the land that he had until then been crossing, i.e. all of Asia excluding China (which was the 'land of the great khan'). Middle and Lesser India were the lands to which he would travel on his return journey, with Middle India being Ethiopia and Lesser India being South East Asia. Such terms continued into much later times, with Odoric also talking about the two Indias. These terms also found their way into maps of the early 16th century, which have *India Intra Gangem* and *India Extra Gangem* to describe India proper (intra Gangem) and China.

Leaving Greater India, Marco entered Mongol lands and made his way to Karakorum, "the first place in which the Tartars established their residence in remote time."[32] In a brief digression on the history of the Tartars, he said that they were a tribe who had no sovereign of their own but were "tributary to a powerful prince, who (as I have been informed) was named in their language, Un-khan, by some thought to have the same significance as Prester John in ours."[33] This chief gradually became more apprehensive of the strength of his subordinates, particularly when Changez Khan became their leader. Marco states that Changez Khan "sent ambassadors to Prester John, . . . demanding his daughter in marriage."[34] Marco's narrative sets the land of Prester John very clearly in central Asia, and not in Ethiopia or in India, where the land came to be located later.

Marco Polo's account is of course most famous for the wealth of details and the details of wealth that he provides about the court at China. For example, officers in the King's service were given engraved tablets as "warrants of command and of government";[35] commanders of a hundred soldiers were given tablets of silver, those of a thousand, of gold or "silver gilt", and those of ten thousand were given gold tablets "bearing the head of a lion". Detailed descriptions were also provided about the capital and the winter residence, named Kanbalu, and the new city of Tai-Du which was being built as the new capital near Kanbalu,[36] as well as of the public court held by the Great Khan. Particularly noteworthy were the vessels used at these public functions – all of gold and silver.

Even though Marco Polo spent most of his years in China following the orders of the Great Khan, and travelling to different parts of the country, he remained primarily interested in commerce. His is therefore the most detailed description of products, trade, trade routes, and exchange systems that we have of the east. Particularly noteworthy are the details that he provided on methods of transport, including wagons and ships. Ships' sizes were described, however, not in tonnage but in the number of bags of pepper that they could carry – indication of the extent of trade in this product within the Asian waters themselves.

Marco was also the first to describe south east Asia, especially Java and Sumatra, in detail. He had been informed that the island of Java was the largest in the world and "being in circuit above 3000 miles. . . . The country abounds with rich commodities. Pepper, nutmegs, . . . and all the other valuable spices and drugs, are the produce of the island; which occasion it to be visited by many ships laden with merchandise."[37] Unlike Java, which was governed by one king, he described Sumatra as an island within which there were eight kingdoms. However, it was equally wealthy, and, like Java, had all kinds of spices and drugs. The produce of these islands "on account of the length of the voyage and the danger of the navigation, are not imported into our country" but were well known in China.[38] Most noteworthy to Marco Polo was that the North Star was invisible in these islands. This was a remarkable addition to the extent of knowledge available to Europe at that time.

Clear from Marco Polo's narrative is that India was a point of reference, but China was still mostly unknown. Information about China and about the countries to which China traded or with which she was associated was both new and extensive. Knowledge about India was accurate when it came to the coasts, but was rather fanciful about anything else. For example, when he spoke of the Tamil Nadu coast, particularly the area around St. Thomas' Mount, he said that the natives of the area were black-skinned, but were "not born of so deep a dye as they afterwards attain by artificial means, esteeming blackness the perfection of beauty. For this purpose, three times every day, they rub the children over with oil of sesame."[39] Difference was also to be seen in the birds, with bats as large as vultures, and vultures as black as crows.[40]

After Marco Polo, Odoric's was probably the first account that described the wealth of Asia, and not just China, in such clear terms. In a Europe that was feudal and land based, where gold was very much a luxury item, to be found only in the possession of kings, descriptions of palaces with walls of gold and dresses of gold would obviously have an immediate and tremendous impact. Any country where such items were to be found, and on such a large scale, obviously had to be explored further, and hopefully traded with, so that some of this wealth could find its way back to Europe – at least to individuals, if not to nations.

While Marco Polo and Odoric described both land and sea routes, there were other travellers and other accounts describing the overland routes across Asia, such as that of Francesco Balducci Pegolotti.[41] He was probably an agent in the service of some mercantile firm of Florence, and apparently travelled around Europe on business concerned with that firm's ventures. It is fairly clear that he never actually travelled into Asia, but his work has a great many chapters devoted to the various ports and the trade routes moving east to west. His point of reference for the beginning of the route started with Tana on the Black Sea. His description of the route involved both time and mode of transport, as, for example, when he said that "from Tana to Gintarchan [Astrakhan] may be twenty-five days with an ox waggon and from ten to twelve with a horse waggon. On the road you will find plenty of *Moccols*, that is to say in *gens d'armes*."[42] He was also the first traveller to mention paper money and its use.

What comes out clearly in his account is the range of goods and the number of duties charged at various points. Products available at Tana included pepper, coarser spices, ginger, and cotton. Constantinople, the bigger market, had "indigo, madder and alum, iron of every kind, tin of every kind, raisins, soap of Venice, dried figs of Majorca and Spain, henna, cumin, sulphur, laudanum of Cyprus, . . ., broken camphor, canvases of all kinds except those of Champagne".[43] This was a world that was remarkable for the number of products, and the many regions that these goods came from, but the system that governed transport and markets were clear to all. The scale was huge, but the method of operation was familiar.

All these travellers belonged to the pre-renaissance age of discovery and cartography. Their reports added to the already existing stories about the wealth of Asia and helped to transfer them from the realm of fantasy and myth to that of reality. The wealth had begun to be described, but subsequent accounts, particularly those from the 16th century onwards, underlined the volume and variety of material wealth available in the east, and made knowledge about this variety more accessible in Europe. Travellers' accounts from that century onwards therefore have a shift in tone, with more emphasis on visible wealth and more details about the society in which this wealth found a place and the nature of that society which could both generate and consume such wealth.

The east had not yet (in 1340 or thereabouts) shifted totally out of Europe. Tana on the Black Sea was apparently well known to Pegalotti as one of the biggest bazaars, but this familiarity was not one that included the place in his world. It was known as the point of entry and exit, so exchange could happen, for it was there that goods from the east came in. It was also, in one sense, the end of the reasonably familiar, for it was from there that merchants set out to go east to get the goods. Equally clear is that what went eastwards was gold and silver, but what came back in was products. Merchants travelled comfortably and in safety but had to be prepared to pay extra to any 'Mongol or Tartar groups' whom they met on the way. Loss of life due to warfare, in the century between Rubruquis and Pegalotti, was apparently no longer a major problem. In a sense, therefore, the east was being much more clearly located in terms of both geography and knowledge of the people. The east was, in other words, beginning to shift more eastwards, and the idea that there were possibly many 'easts' was beginning to make its appearance – something that, in the 19th century and later, took concrete shape as 'Near' East, 'Middle' East, and 'Far' East.

Yet another account that is of importance is Friar Jordanus' *Mirabilia Descripta*. Jordanus was sent out as Bishop of "Columbum", probably Quilon in Kerala, in the early decades of the 14th century. One letter dated 1324 talks about how he left Tabriz (in Persia) to go to 'Cathay', but first left for Columbum with four Franciscan missionaries. A storm drove them to Thana, now a suburb of Mumbai, and they were received by Nestorian Christians there. Jordanus set out to go to Bharuch in Gujarat but was detained at Sopara, also now in Mumbai.[44] Around 1330 he was apparently in Columbum.[45]

Unlike Odoric and Marco Polo, Jordanus' account went back to the 'marvels' of the east. But for him, these marvels began as soon as he set out on his travels. For instance, in his description of the Mediterranean Sea, he said that "in the bottom of the sea there is a horrid kind of whirlpool, from which the water cometh forth so wondrous dark that even the fishes nowhere dare to come near it."[46] This does take us back to the Charybdis of earlier legends, but is a fitting start to his Mirabilia. Every country that the Friar visited was distinguished by marvels – so "Armenia the Greater" had "a mountain of excessive height and immense extent, on which Noah's Ark is said to have rested";[47] in Persia, in the city of Tabriz, "dew never falls from heaven; nor doth it rain in summer as in most parts it doth, but they water artificially everything that is grown for man's food."[48] Reaching India he was clearly in "another world; for the men and women be all black".[49] Not just the people, but the land itself was "worthy to be noted with wonder; for there are no springs, no rivers, no ponds; nor does it ever rain, except during three months, viz., between the middle of May and the middle of August; (wonderful!) not withstanding this, the soil is most kindly and fertile."[50]

This 'other world' was different from all the lands that he was familiar with in every possible way. So, fruits, trees, birds, animals were all 'marvellous' things. Particularly wonderful was of course the banyan tree "which sendeth forth roots from high up, which gradually grow down to the ground and enter it, and then wax into trunks like the main trunk, forming as it were an arch. . . . 'Tis marvellous!"[51] As much as the trees and the birds, the animals were proof of India being another world. So there were "coquodriles, which are vulgarly called *calcatix*; some of them be so big that they be bigger than the biggest horse. . . . This animal has it were a coat of mail,"[52] and elephants, which were the largest and gentlest of creatures until angered.

What comes out clearly in Jordanus is the considerable accuracy of his descriptions, but he apparently felt the need to couch his descriptions within the structure of the marvellous. Even though by his time India was known enough that a Bishop could be appointed for Quilon, and so was a recognisable world inhabited by Christians, the distance from the known lands of Christendom required it to be depicted as fabulous. Thus, unlike Odoric and Marco Polo, his is an account that is very firmly part of the medieval world of wonder, and not the emerging world of concrete description and understanding. Perhaps the difference in these different writings is best brought out in his own words: "every thing indeed is a marvel in this India! Verily it is quite another world!"[53]

The point about all of these accounts is that they displayed a definite familiarity and an accuracy of description. The lands that they described were now no longer mythical or fantastic, but fabulous or marvellous. Descriptions were still located within the earlier framework of Greater and Lesser India (Marco Polo and Jordanus) or Upper India and Inland India (Odoric). For Jordanus, Lesser India was from Sind and Makran down along the coast till Malabar, Greater India for him extended from Malabar eastwards and included Champa, while India Tertia was the east of Africa. Marco Polo reversed Jordanus to make Greater India extend from the Coromandel coast to Makran, and Lesser India from Coromandel to Champa; Abyssinia was Middle India. For Odoric, Upper India was China, Inland India was from Persia to India, and then there was India proper. These descriptions of the 13th century continued even into the 15th, but with some changes, for the 15th-century Italian traveller Conti declared that India was divided into three parts: the first from Persia to the Indus, the second from the Indus to the Ganges, and the third, everything beyond. A shift from the fabulous to the real was beginning, but the real was not yet relegated to 'mundane', for the wealth alone made it clear that these lands were not ordinary. But greater knowledge was clearly needed, so that this wealth could make its way back to their own worlds.

Notes

1 Henry Yule (tr. and ed.), *Cathay and the Way Thither: Being a Collection of Medieval Notices of China*, Vol. 2, New Series, London: Hakluyt Society, 1913, p. 176.
2 Ronald Latham (tr. and ed.), *Marco Polo: The Travels*, Penguin Books, 1958, Introduction, p. 11.
3 Sir Alfred William Pollard (ed.), *The Travels of Sir John Mandeville, with Three Narratives in Illustration of It: The Voyage of Johannes de Plano Carpini, the Journal of William de Rubruquis, and the Journal of Friar Odoric from Hakluyt's "Navigations, Voyages and Discoveries"*, London: Macmillan & Co, 1900 (henceforth cited as Mandeville, followed by specific narrative), Narrative of Carpini, p. 214.
4 Robert Silverberg, *The Realm of Prester John*, First Published, 1972; Republished London: Phoenix Press, 2001, p. 90.
5 Mandeville, op.cit., p. 217.
6 In the 20th-century children's stories *The Chronicles of Narnia*, written by C.S. Lewis, we have, in one book, meetings with the "Monopods" – creatures who have only one foot!
7 Silverberg, op.cit., p. 92.
8 Mandeville, Carpini, p. 215.
9 Ibid., William of Rubruquis, p. 266.
10 See Mandeville, Ibid., p. 109 and *passim*, where it is said that India consisted of over '5000 isles', and that "In every isle is great plenty of cities, and of towns."
11 Ibid., Rubruquis, p. 273.
12 Ibid., p. 106.
13 Ibid.
14 Silverberg, op.cit., p. 102.
15 Ibid., Carpini, p. 237.
16 Ibid., Rubruquis, p. 266.
17 Ibid., Carpini, p. 216.
18 Ibid., Rubruquis, p. 273.
19 Henry Yule (tr. and ed.), *Cathay and the Way Thither: Being a Collection of Medieval Notices of China*, Vol. 1, London: Hakluyt Society, 1866, Friar Odoric of Pordenone, p. 44.
20 Ibid., pp. 48–49.
21 Ibid., pp. 50–51.
22 Ibid., pp. 54–56.
23 It is because of this, the link with Alexander, that it is suggested that he meant Thatta rather than Thana.
24 The word 'Mobar' appears to be a corruption of Ma'abar, the name of the Sultanate that was established when the Khalji armies from north India defeated the Pandya rulers of Madurai. The Ma'abar coast therefore referred to the southeastern coast of India in present-day Tamil Nadu.
25 Ibid., p. 81.
26 Ibid., p. 77.
27 Ibid., pp. 85, 88.
28 Pollard, op.cit., p. 335.
29 Yule, *Cathay . . .*, p. 92.
30 Pollard, op.cit., p. 337.
31 Ibid., p. 349.
32 *The Travels of Marco Polo: The Venetian* with an Introduction by John Masefield, first published, London, 1931; New Delhi: Asian Educational Services Reprint, 2003, p. 115.

33 Ibid., pp. 116–117.
34 Ibid., p. 119. This is probably the source of Mandeville's statement that the king of Cathay always married into the family of Prester John.
35 Ibid., p. 161.
36 Ibid., pp. 166, 172.
37 Travels of Marco Polo, op. cit., p. 334.
38 Ibid., pp. 337–338.
39 Ibid., p. 365. Sesame oil is still used, but has nothing to do with changing the colour of the skin!
40 Ibid., p. 362.
41 Henry Yule, *Cathay and the Way Thither*, Vol. 2, London: Hakluyt Society, 1866, pp. 279–308.
42 Ibid.
43 Ibid.
44 Henry Yule (tr. and ed.), *Mirabilia Descripta, the Wonders of the East, by Friar Jordanus (circa 1330)*, London: Hakluyt Society, 1863, Preface, p. vi.
45 Ibid., p. vii.
46 Ibid., p. 1.
47 Ibid., p. 3.
48 Ibid., pp. 7–8.
49 Ibid., p. 12.
50 Ibid.
51 Ibid., p. 17. The description of the Indian banyan is also found in Milton's *Paradise Lost*.
52 Ibid., p. 19.
53 Ibid., p. 37.

3 Exploring the east

The centuries after the travels of the friars saw an explosion in the numbers of travellers out of Europe, and the heralding of what has been called the age of discovery. An immense curiosity about the world and its multiple dimensions – one part of which was science – became the hallmark of, particularly, the period from the 15th century onwards. The role of Vasco da Gama, Christopher Columbus, Ferdinand Magellan, and others in the course of the century, in opening up different parts of the world to the European gaze and entry, has been extensively documented. However, they were only the later and more famous of the travellers of the century, for before them, people like Nicolo Conti and Athanasius Nikitin had travelled extensively in Asia.

Conti was instrumental in showing the Latin-speaking world the extent of trade within the continent, and the place of Chinese products in this trade, and Nikitin presumably did the same for the Russian-speaking world. What is clear is that, much more than ever before, people were moving out of their enclosed spaces, and looking out at the world. Of course, not everyone could, or wanted to, travel, but an audience for the accounts of travellers was definitely growing. The armchair traveller was clearly beginning to emerge from the shadows, and the printing press played its part in the development of this audience. As the age of discovery progressed, and as the emphasis on 'knowledge' began to steadily increase, the travelogues also began to reflect the new mentality. The account of Nicolo Conti (1385–1469) was perhaps among the earliest in which this change was manifested.

Nicolo Conti, a Venetian, spent a considerable part of his life in Asia, and apparently converted to Islam at some point during his stay there. His account of his travels and his stay in the east was in the nature of penance for having converted, and was the method for his reacceptance within the fold of the Church. He did not write the account himself, but dictated it to the papal secretary Poggio Bracciolini in 1439, who then wrote it in Latin.[1]

Conti's time in Asia had seen the great Chinese expeditions under the leadership of Admiral Zheng-he, and it has been suggested that it was through Conti, and his contacts with the Chinese chronicler Ma-huan, that Chinese geographical knowledge spread to the west, to spark off the Renaissance. The claim is questionable, but what is clear in the account is the detailed knowledge of the interior (especially the south) of India, as well as the curiosity in Europe to get first-hand information. Equally clear is the fact that a considerable amount of information had already been collected – enough that earlier accounts could be more critically assessed. Poggio at one point remarked that many things were 'reported of the inhabitants of India' by ancient writers 'by common repute', but it was clear that much of this information was false, and part of the value of the account that he was then collating was its accuracy.

In the process of dictating and finally putting together the text of Conti's travels, it is rather difficult to determine the extent of re-organisation actually done by Poggio. We also do not know whether it was Conti's or Poggio's views about the past writers that finally found its way into the text. That is probably a question best left to others to decide, but what is clear is that there is no mention of either Marco Polo or Odoric in the narrative. On the other hand, the accuracy of the account of Conti is stressed, as one who had lived and worked in the east and therefore was a qualified observer. Travel narratives, with Conti, now began to acquire a dimension of accuracy stressed through the fact of the writer being an eye witness. The experiences of the traveller had always played a role in the stories he had to tell, but now, the traveller was beginning to move from just a storyteller to a chronicler providing knowledge. Travel was therefore beginning to move into the realm of legitimate activity, even if not dedicated to a pilgrimage.

Still, some of the older ideas, as for example, about divisions of territory, continue into Conti's text. As said earlier, for Conti, India consisted of three parts – the first from Persia to the Indus, the second from the Indus to the Ganges, and the third beyond the Ganges, particularly China (what Odoric had called Upper India). Civility increased the further inward one went, and so the inhabitants of furthest India, China, were the most civil and humane – a total contrast to early descriptions of the Mongol lands of China.[2]

It is possible that such divisions were the result of an even earlier legacy, which recognised the existence of three continents[3] – Europe, Africa, and Asia – and acknowledged Asia as the largest. But in Asia, there was primarily India; and so, Asia had to be defined with reference to India, as divisions of India. Therefore, it was only now that very specific descriptions of India, as opposed to the fanciful writings of earlier, began to emerge.

Unlike Odoric and Marco Polo, Conti never reached China, but he did travel inland in India, and beyond, to southeast Asia. As a visitor to the southern kingdom of Vijayanagar, his account of that kingdom has long been regarded as an important source for the wealth of information that is available in the text. Where Odoric talked of the wealth of China, in terms of both money and products, Conti did the same with Vijayanagar. His account provided, also for the first time, a clear description of law and the practices of justice, and ideas of kingship. India had always been counted as civilised; now an element of 'safety' was added, for here was a kingdom with recognisable features of administration and justice. Wealth made it exotic, while government and legal structures made it understandable. What is also noticeable is that from now onwards, all accounts make specific mention of the systems of justice prevalent in India, in contrast to the later colonial perceptions. India, in these emerging descriptions, was a land which seemed to have everything – the calendar, coinage, military technology, paper and writing, languages, slavery, and of course wealth. These descriptions tended to reinforce what had always been assumed about India.

Like Marco Polo, Conti too described southeast Asia. According to him, there were two Javas, "distinguished from each other by the names of the Greater and the Less. They are distant from the continent one month's sail and lie within one hundred miles of each other."[4] He was careful to point to the differences in practices in India and in these islands, the most marked of which was cannibalism. It is noteworthy that cannibalism finds mention in all three of the accounts so far discussed that mention Java, i.e. those of Marco Polo, Odoric, and Conti.

Conti began the process that continued till well into the 18th century, of stating that India required nothing from Europe. What she did need could be sourced from other parts of Asia, with which there were long-established contacts of both trade and diplomacy. The European entrant was possibly a curiosity because of the colour of his skin, and perhaps because of the language/s that he spoke, but finally, merely a buyer, and so to some extent, a supplicant, in that the Europeans had to wait with other newcomers to gain access to the products that they wanted. In order to get these products, they had to approach the courts and the kings through intermediaries of many kinds. The need to identify intermediaries, as well as the increasing curiosity about different social systems, led to descriptions of society in many of the chronicles from this time on. It is possibly in this context that one needs to read Conti's description of the way in which the Asians regarded the Europeans. He mentioned that "the inhabitants of India call us Franks; they have two eyes, we one," which he said was an Indian expression of disdain for the ignorance of European visitors.[5] We therefore need to understand the travel accounts themselves differently and focus on the fact that, post 15th century, all accounts provide information about people, castes and society in general before going into descriptions of the courts.

Conti represented, as said previously, the first stage of the emphasis on eyewitness accounts and accuracy. With the opening up of the sea route to India, and the establishment of Portuguese colonialism in Asia, there began increased access to the Eastern lands, beyond the known 'holy lands'. Many took advantage of this access, both out of a desire to see the world, and to try and make a profit. Such profit would ideally be real, in the sense that they could make some money out of it; but there were also gains that could be made in acquiring a reputation as a traveller, with true stories to tell.

Ludovico di Varthema[6] was one such traveller, who seems to have travelled just out of a desire to do so – an early case of itchy feet! Other than the fact that he travelled to Asia early in the 16th century, and that he was originally from Bologna but later settled in Venice, we have no details about his life. Leaving Europe in 1502, he travelled through Arabia and Persia and then went on to India and the East Indies. Unlike the new Portuguese-empire-associated travellers, however, he travelled by the old route – across the Mediterranean to Egypt, then by boat down the Red Sea, then by land and by sea to Persia, and finally by sea to India and Sumatra. Like Conti, he also professed Islam for a while, but apparently not long enough for him to be required to do any penance on his return to Europe.

Varthema also marks the beginning of a new kind of traveller, one who looked for new experiences: so, he remarked on reaching Alexandria, that he left the place "as being well-known to all, and, entering the Nile, arrived at Cairo."[7] Extending the kind of narrative initiated by Conti, his point too was to record that which was unknown to his countrymen and therefore to add to their knowledge.

Part of the knowledge that was being offered now was skin colour, produce, and distances. For the last, the measurement was not in terms of mileage but time, something that was then probably much more important. (However, it should be remembered that he was not the first to do so, as both Pegalotti and Conti had done the same earlier.) Places were thus described as being forty days' journey by camel, or three days sailing. Details about produce found along the way and about food available for the traveller were also given. One can therefore also see the beginning of what later developed into what can perhaps be termed the full-fledged 'trade account' – travelogues that focussed on prices, goods, and suppliers.

Particularly important to Varthema was skin colour. At every place that he passed, he specifically mentioned the colour of the people he saw, and remarked that they ranged from tawny to black, but that there were very few white skins. As with the friars, so with him, there is no sense of superiority linked to colour, but we get an addition – according to him, the white skin was a source of attraction to the women of the east. In a couple of instances, he attributed his escape from trouble and perhaps death to his skin colour; for upper class or royal women, he declared, negotiated his freedom because they were fascinated by the 'white man'. With him, therefore, is introduced one of the themes that then became a constant in such travelogues, that of the sexuality – repressed, therefore searching for avenues of expression – of the eastern woman. There is not yet that prurient interest with the harem that comes through in later accounts, but there is undoubtedly a fascination and the underlining of the difference among the women of the east and west.

As with earlier travellers, so with Varthema, once he arrived in India, there was a sense, not quite of familiarity, but of greater comfort. India did not need to be introduced to his readers, but the bewildering variety of people in that land had to be described. So, it is only with India that we find him giving information about society – in the other places that he visited, he described the nobility to a limited extent, but focussed mainly on the group he called the 'Mamelukes' – the warriors. Otherwise, what comes through is a sense of

42 Exploring the east

large numbers of people, but not a social organisation that he could clearly identify. With India, on the other hand, the organisational structure of society was clear, and clearly different from anything else within his sphere of experience until then. So, he said

> the first class of pagans are called *Brahmins*. The second are *Naeri*,[8] who are the same as gentle folks amongst us; and these are obliged to bear sword and shield or bows or lances. When they go through the street, if they did not carry arms, they would no longer be gentlemen. The third class of pagans are called *Tiva*, who are artisans. The fourth class are called *Mechua*, and these are fishermen. The fifth class, are called *Poliar*, who collect pepper wine and nuts. The sixth class are called *Hirava*, and these plant and gather in rice. These last two classes of people may not approach either the *Naeri* or the *Brahmins* within fifty paces, unless they have been called by them.[9]

Already in the early 16th century, information on India's caste system was making its way back to Europe.

Where Conti provided information about commodities and prices, Varthema described society and people. Both these travellers espoused Islam while in Asia. What one gets is a sense of expediency – that as travellers in strange lands, they had to do what was necessary to survive, and public acceptance of a religion was part of the survival strategy, and therefore to be seen as such, without any stigma being attached to it. This attitude seems rather strange in the light of the European experience with the Crusades and with the Mongols, but at least for these two travellers, it was not a major issue. Whether this was because there was, as yet, no real competition over resources, or a confrontation in political terms despite the inherited legacy of the Crusades and the advancing Ottoman power, is something that is none too clear. However, what is certain is that for these two travellers, at any rate, espousing a particular religion at a specific point of time was expediency, not commitment. Religion was a marker of identity but does not seem to have been seen by them as the only marker. This attitude is particularly striking given that this is also the century in which the Portuguese empire with its strong bent towards conversion was also beginning to be established.

Varthema's account gives us the initial stages of the establishment of Portuguese power in Asia, as is clear particularly in his description of Ormuz. As said earlier, Varthema took the older route to get to India, i.e. partly by land and partly by sea. In another sense too, he marks a point of change, for later travellers were often in some sense associated with the various companies that came to India. Conti and Varthema were individual travellers, without the force of company or state behind them. (The two famous French accounts of the 17th century, those of Tavernier and Bernier, were not linked to the French company of course, but cannot be included in the same category as Varthema.)

The establishment of power generated a fresh kind of documentation which obviously included the apparatus of empire, but also involved movement of officials of the Company in different parts of the emerging empire. Many of these officials recorded their experiences, and one of the earliest of such writings is that of Duarte Barbosa.[10] With Barbosa one moves into yet another kind of travelogue – the official one. The Portuguese official presence obviously generated both employment and writing of different kinds, and Barbosa's account is a good example of both. An employee of the Portuguese Estado da India, he was in India from about 1500 till about 1516/17. He was one of the first to learn the local language and while employed as the 'writer', he was apparently much in demand for his linguistic ability.

As an account written at the time that the Portuguese were establishing themselves in Asia, Barbosa's naturally has a great many details about the Portuguese conquests – and about the problems that came in the wake of these conquests, both within the Portuguese official sphere, and from the Asian (especially Indian) kings. For instance, he was apparently part of the group that questioned the wisdom of establishing the centre of the Portuguese empire at Goa, arguing that Cannanore and Cochin were much more suitable, both from the point of view of friendly kings and the availability of products for trade.

Like Varthema, he gave descriptions of people and the countries, but also added much information about trade. Barbosa naturally gave a detailed account of the new route to India around the Cape of Good Hope. As one of the early travellers along this route, but also one who had to record details of the journey for the benefit of those who would follow, there had to be information provided about anchorages, food and water and the friendliness or otherwise of the natives. Therefore, unlike Varthema, who particularly mentioned the colour of people, Barbosa talked of the products available and the methods of purchase. Underlying his account, however, is also the sense of empire. So, for example, when talking of the port of Sofala, he took care to point out both, that the Portuguese had a fort nearby, and that the king of Sofala was subject to the Portuguese king. He talked of the use of coir in the boats there, but did not mention the lack of iron, unlike Friar Odoric who had particularly remarked on the absence of this metal in the vessels of the Arabian Sea. Whether this means that iron had subsequently begun to be used on these boats, or just that he did not care to mention this, as being irrelevant to his concerns, is uncertain. Barbosa was far more concerned with the merchandise which he said was carried in "small vessels . . . from the kingdoms of Quiloa, Mombasa, and Melynde, bringing many cotton cloths, some spotted and others white and blue, also some of silk, and many small beads, grey, red, and yellow, which things come to the said kingdom of Cambaya[11] in other greater ships."[12] In return, ivory was sent across to Gujarat. Here is the first indication of one aspect of the trade across the Arabian Sea, of cloth and probably carnelian beads leaving India and ivory going in. Slightly later in the account, he described the trade from the Red Sea to Calicut, where "much copper, quicksilver, verdigris, saffron, rosewater, scarlet cloth, silks . . . and divers others goods are sent to India, also with much gold and silver."[13]

As early as Barbosa's time, there was also apparently a reaction to the Portuguese entry, for he said that the people of Sofala had begun a new industry, of reweaving Cambay cloth "as a remedy after we had perceived that our people were taking from them the trade of the *zambucos* [small country trade ships]."[14]

Following the trend that had already begun, he also mentioned skin colour but very briefly, merely saying that many were "black, and some of them tawny".[15] However, he was far more interested in the clothes they wore and the kinds of food they ate. Even in the description of the clothes, one can see the focus on acquiring knowledge about products, especially cloth. He therefore remarked on the caps that some of the people wore which he said were "dyed in grain in chequers and other woollen clothes in many tints, also camlets and other silks".[16] Once again there is visible a sense of amazement that even those who were fairly ordinary people could wear silks, which in Europe were the prerogative of only the wealthy.

Stories about the land of Prester John clearly continued to exist, but it is possibly with Barbosa that his realm began to move out of India into Africa. He said that

> Travelling inland from the position of these same Moorish towns, [Sofala and Malindi] there is a very great realm, that of the Preste Joam, which the Moors call Abexy [Abyssinia]. It is very widespread and abounds in fair lands: . . . he holds many kingdoms around subject to him. . . . well peopled with many cities, towns and villages. They are black men with good figures, and they have horses in abundance which they use.[17]

They were Christians, of course, and had been since the time of St. Thomas, but unlike the Christians of Europe, they had three baptisms – by water (like the Europeans) and by fire and blood.[18]

From the land of Prester John, moving north towards the Red Sea and Persia, more familiar ground was obviously being approached. So, for instance, in the descriptions of Ormuz and Basra, details were provided about the clothing, the kinds of weaponry carried, and the quality of the food. The point of reference for Barbosa, whether in urbanity or gallantry or food, was Spain, but there were things found that did not exist in Spain. So even Ormuz, which was otherwise a barren island with only salt available, had access to riches through trade, and not a very distant trade, at that.

'Curiosities' of course continued to exist, as with the sea horses which came out on land to graze and which had tusks of ivory which were whiter and harder than those of elephants. Wild elephants existed in great number, but they could not be tamed by the people there, even though the people were reasonably familiar with weapons of different kinds. They had the technology but not the expertise to domesticate animals. The sense of an alien landscape – alien both in flora and fauna and in customs of the people – appears to be one of the major underlying themes of Barbosa's descriptions.

India remained familiar ground, but with the addition for Barbosa, of it being imperial domain. Descriptions therefore referred not just to wealth but also to politics, for negotiations had to be made with the local rulers, to firmly establish the Portuguese. Given that the Portuguese entered through the south-west coast of India, descriptions of Malabar are naturally much more detailed in his account. However, as with Varthema, a sense of first, the existence of a clearly definable structure of kingship and governance, and therefore, second, the possibility of dealing with such structures without too much trouble, comes out very clearly. The familiarity of India was now being reinforced through descriptions of familiar institutions of power and governance.

If Barbosa's was a travelogue of the emergence of early (pre-industrial) colonialism, the first English account, that of Ralph Fitch, in true Elizabethan style, was one that looked at the prospect of profit alone, without the establishment of an empire. It is an account that both went back to an earlier time and took travel accounts to a new level, in the sense that there are elaborate descriptions, but also, for the first time, descriptions of the interior of India and the routes across the subcontinent and beyond.

Given the fact of colonialism, English-language documents have generally been regarded as of supreme importance in the Indian context. But it should be remembered that the English travellers were rather later arrivals on the Asian scene. Just as, in Europe, the English went into exploration rather later, but then made up for lost time, so also, in the matter of travel to India, they came late, but made up for their tardiness. One of the first Englishmen was a Jesuit priest, Father Stephen, who came early in the 16th century to the west coast, but given his calling, his concerns were primarily religious. He was the author of a work called the *Christa Purana*, the first rendering of the Bible into Marathi, and also one of the first works in Marathi by a foreigner. This work can in no sense be called a travelogue. The honour of writing the first travel account of India and parts further east in English belongs to Ralph Fitch. While some of the importance given to Fitch's account is because of it being the first, the fact of his being the only member of his party to return alive to England to report probably made him equally important. (It further of course reinforced the importance of the traveller who returned to tell his tale.)

In about 1583, the joint boards of the Levant and Muscovy Companies chose Ralph Fitch, John Newberry, John Eldred, William Leedes, and James Story to travel to India. Fitch was presumably one of the free merchants who had money to spend on going to the east. Eldred was a merchant who was familiar with Baghdad, having spent two years there, Leedes was a jeweller, Story a painter, and Newberry a merchant who knew Arabic, and had earlier travelled to Tripoli and Syria. According to one account, they were chosen

46 *Exploring the east*

because they were "men of singular courage",[19] and such men "were known and welcome enough at the Mogul court."[20] They left England in 1583 and achieved the rather doubtful honour of arriving in India as prisoners of the Portuguese. They had been arrested in Ormuz on suspicion of their being spies of the pretender to the Portuguese crown, Don Antonio.

Descriptions of the trade with the east begin with Ormuz itself. An island which produced nothing but salt, it was nevertheless one of the great emporia of the world, wherein it was possible to find "merchants of all Nations, and many Moores and Gentiles".[21] The goods traded in included "all sorts of spices, drugs, silke, cloth of silke, fine tapestries of Persia, great store of pearles . . . and many horses of Persia".[22] Shortly after, the party was imprisoned, and taken to India, and the account that Fitch gives of the market of Chaul is also replete with details of the merchandise to be seen there – "all sorts of spices and drugges, silkes and cloth of silke, sandales, Elephants teeth, and much China work, and much sugar ".[23]

Fitch was taken to Goa and managed to escape and make his way inland, to go to Burhanpur, and from there into the Mughal empire. From this point on, one can see once again, a juxtaposition of the ordinary and the fantastic, interspersed with descriptions of the people and the customs of the country. Equally important is the fact that from his account onwards, the two aspects – the ordinary and the fantastic – run parallel to each other. For example, when describing Burhanpur, he began with the cotton cloth produced in the region, and then went on to a description of child marriages, sati and a description of a wedding procession, and ended with a brief description of the size of the kingdom. Similarly, in his description of Patna, there is naturally a detailed description of the Ganges, but there was also a fascination with a set of scenes with which he was totally unfamiliar – for instance, he talked of the monsoon, the width of the river, and the mosquitoes infesting India, in almost the same sentence. The world that he was describing was clearly very distant from that occupied by his English readers, so what he brought to them was a sense of 'adventure' and 'foreignness', while they were secure and comfortable at home. In one way, he was also pointing to the lack of security and comfort in India and, therefore, to the intrepidity of the traveller. This idea of security (or rather, its lack) was reaffirmed through trade, for the problems that the East India Company had with local Indian rulers were widely reported and discussed in England.

The size of the Mughal empire was something that amazed all travellers to India. Most descriptions specifically mentioned the provinces of Cambay (Gujarat) and Bengal, and remarked that within this immense territory was produced everything that anyone could possibly need. What comes out clearly is that, contrary to later images of India as a country that 'lived in its villages', cities were a crucial part of the economy of the country. All the travellers were impressed with the size of the cities, which were considerably larger than any in Europe at that time. And, of course, the range of production was immense, as was the wealth of internal trade. Fitch said that the distance between Agra and Fatehpur Sikri was twelve miles, "and all the way [was] a market of victuals & other things, as full as though a man were still in a towne, and so many people as if a man were in a market."[24]

All the accounts give details of the size of the kingdom, and the size of the cities in it. According to one traveller, the 'Empire of this Mogor' was "exceeding great, containing the countries of Bengala, Cambaya, Mendao [Mandu], and others, comprehended by some under the name of Industan."[25] William Hawkins, who was at Jahangir's court, said that the Empire was divided into "five Great Kingdoms, the first named Pengab [Punjab], the chiefe Citie whereof is Lahor; the second Bengala, and Sonargham [Sonargaon] the mother Citie; the third, Malua [Malwa], the chiefe Seat Vagain [Ujjain]; the fourth Deckan, in which Bramport [Burhanpur] is principall: and so is Amadavar [Ahmedabad] in the fifth kingdome, which is Cambaya."[26] Yet another traveller, Thomas Coryat, took twenty days walking from Lahore to Agra "through such a delicate and even tract of ground as I never saw before, and doubt whether the like bee to be found within the whole circumference of the habitable world. . . . [The road was lined with] a row of trees on each side of this way where people doe travel, extending itself from the townes end of Lahore to the townes end of Agra."[27] Given the size of the countries from which these travellers came, the extent of the kingdom of the Mughals was obviously instantly striking.

Geographical extent had to be matched by wealth (yet again). Where Ralph Fitch went into details about the number, size, and extent of the trade of the various cities that he passed through on his travels through India, Thomas Coryat described only one thing in detail: the weighing ceremony, in which the emperor was weighed against gold, quicksilver, silk, perfumes, copper, drugs, ghee, and some other articles, in order of cost, and the goods that were weighed were then distributed among the poor.[28] Quite apart from the weighing ceremony itself, the list of goods is indicative of the range of produce and the quantities that were produced.[29] It was stated that the King's revenue amounted to "fiftie Crou [crore] of rupias; every Crou is one hundred Leckes [lakhs], and every Lecke a hundred thousand Rupias; all which is . . . fiftie millions of pounds."[30] Included in this description of wealth were, of course, elephants. William Finch[31] had talked of the number of elephants that Akbar had in his elephant stables, and of the number used in war. Elephants were, after all, a costly item, and to be able to look after thirty thousand elephants on a regular basis would have to be a costly affair! It is mentioned that Emperor Jahangir's daily expenses amounted to "fiftie thousand Rupias, for his owne person, as apparel, victuals, and other household expences, with the feeding of sundry sorts of beasts, and of some few Elephants; his expences on his women by the day amount to thirtie thousand Rupias."[32]

With Fitch, Coryat, Hawkins, and Finch, one can see a greater engagement with the entirety of India, rather than with just the coast. Fitch was unique in that he was the earliest European traveller to move extensively through the country. From Goa he went overland through the territories of the sultanate of Bijapur to Golconda, then moving northwards went through Burhanpur and Ujjain to Agra. He then travelled along the Ganges into Bengal and from there sailed to Pegu and Siam. On his return from Siam he came back to Bengal and then sailed directly through the Bay to Ceylon (Sri Lanka) and then to the Malabar coast and back to Goa. By sea again he went from Goa to Chaul and then retraced his footsteps.

For him, the levels of unfamiliarity increased exponentially when he left India. Pegu had the Portuguese, and it had elephants and boats, but the language was strange, the customs were stranger still, and the society had not even been described, not even to the limited extent that Indian society had been. The old idea of India being civilised and surrounded by less civilised lands was reaffirmed. India remained safe and open to a modicum of understanding, or at least description, which could then lead to greater knowledge. Perhaps more important to him was the fact of India being governed with a very identifiable form and system of government.

However, older forms of writing that focussed primarily on the coasts continued, as for example, in the account of John Huyghen van Linschoten, a Dutchman who travelled to India in the Portuguese fleet, and arrived in Goa in September 1583. He stayed in Goa for five years, returning finally to Holland in 1592. His work was published within a few years of his return, in 1596.[33]

Linschoten's work has been seen as being valuable mainly for the details that he provided about Portuguese operations and methods in Asian waters, which he could observe at close quarters as a result of his travelling with the Portuguese fleet. It is probably significant that, on his return, he advised his countrymen to land at Java first, as the Portuguese did not have a hold on that island (which was what the Dutch finally did). He too, went into considerable detail about the people of the places he visited. As Carpini had done some three centuries earlier, he described the people he saw, but unlike Carpini, and continuing with the trend begun with Varthema, his descriptions focussed on skin colour rather than physical features. The island of Mozambique, an important port of call for the Portuguese fleet, was described as "inhabited by Mahometans, and they are all most white apparelled in silk and clothes of cotton wooll: their women weare bracelets of gold and precious stones about their neckes and armès: they have great quantities of silver workes, and are not so browne as the men."[34] He then described the mestizos, the people of mixed Portuguese and Asian blood, saying that they were "also esteemed and accounted as Portingals",[35] and distinguished them from the "natural born people of the countrie", who were black. A little later, he said that the people of Ormuz were "white like the Persians". North of Mozambique were areas which were inhabited by Christians and Muslims, as well as by those whom he called 'pagans' – not belonging to either religion, but all of who were mostly black. In India, those who lived "upon the hill, called Ballagatte" (the Ghat areas of the coast), were of a 'yellow colour', while those who lived along the coast itself were "blacker, their statures, visages and limmes are altogether like men of Europa, and those of the coast of Malabar . . . are as blacke as pitch."[36] As he travelled further east, he remarked on the similarity of features between the Chinese and the people of "Aracan, Pegu and Siam", the only difference being that they were rather browner than the Chinese, and blacker than the natives of Bengal.[37] As pointed out previously, his focus was on skin colour, but as a marker of difference, not of inferiority. This is particularly clear in his mention of the mestizos being included among the Portuguese, and apparently having equal status, in marked contrast to the attitude to the 'half-breed' of later times. A rather noticeable feature is that he does make use of the word "Moor" fairly regularly, but unlike later writers, he appears to have used the word as a synonym for 'black', not Muslim. (It is interesting that in the same century Shakespeare used the word with the same connotation when he described Othello.)

Like other travellers of the same period, he too described the volume and variety of products of the trade of Asia in great detail, and remarked in particular on the overland caravan trade between Basra and Aleppo, in which merchants of all countries, including 'France, Britain and Venice'[38] participated. India was described as "very fruitfull of Ryce, Pease, and other graines, Butter and oyle of Indian Nuttes" – the only thing he missed was olive oil. He was among the earliest to point out the medicinal value of many of the herbs found in Asia, something that formed a valuable item of trade in the 17th century.

Throughout the 16th century, knowledge about the eastern lands steadily increased. What did not change was the centrality of India as recognisable, open to strangers, and therefore welcoming; but India also had its own oddities, which now needed to be made more explicit. In many ways India became much more central, not to the imagination but to functioning. India became a base from where further explorations east could be made. This naturally meant that India had to be better described, and that India became the point of comparison for both east and west. In the process perhaps the original 'wonder' of India began to be lost and the country taken much more for granted. As the further east became better understood, both the east and India began to be objectified.

Notes

1 Michèle Guéret-Laferté, *De l'Inde: Les voyages en Asie de Niccolò De'Conti*, Belgium: Brepols, 2004.
2 Supriya Chaudhuri, "The Idea of India", Paper presented (in Italian as *L'Idea dell'India*), at International Conference on Oriente e Occidente nel Rinascimento, XIX Convegno di Istituto Francesco Petrarca, Chianciano-Pienza, Italy, July 2007.
3 As, for example, in the 13th-century account of the English historian William of Malmesbury. See infra Chapter 1.
4 Major, pp. 15–16.
5 It would perhaps also be interesting to look at the ways in which, in earlier times within India, the word *mleccha* was used.

50 *Exploring the east*

6 John Winter Jones (tr.) and George Percy Badger (ed.), *The Travels of Ludovico di Varthema in Egypt, Syria, Arabia Deserta and Arabia Felix, in Persia, India and Ethiopia, A.S. 1503–1508*, London: Hakluyt Society, 1863.
7 Ibid., p. 5.
8 This presumably refers to the Nairs of Kerala. It should also be remembered that his account of society was limited to the coast, and to Malabar in particular.
9 Ibid., pp. 141–142.
10 M.L. Dames (tr. and ed.), *The Book of Duarte Barbosa*, 2 Vols., first published London: Hakluyt Society, 1918–1921; New Delhi: Asian Educational Services Second Reprint, 2002.
11 The port of Cambay, but the name was used to refer to the Sultanate of Gujarat as a whole.
12 Ibid., Vol. 1, pp. 7–8.
13 Ibid., p. 47.
14 Ibid., p. 8. This is also perhaps the earliest mention of the reaction to the Portuguese methods in Asian and African waters.
15 Ibid.
16 Ibid.
17 Ibid., p. 40.
18 Ibid., p. 41.
19 Ram Chandra Prasad, *Early English Travellers in India*, New Delhi: Motilal Banarsidass, 1965, 2nd rev. ed. 1980, p. 24.
20 J. Courtney Locke, *The First Englishmen in India*, London: Broadway House, 1930, p. 9, cited in ibid.
21 J. Horton Riley, *Ralph Fitch: England's Pioneer to India*, London: J. Fisher Unwin, 1899, p. 55.
22 Ibid., p. 56. (Henceforth cited as Ralph Fitch).
23 Ibid., p. 59.
24 Ibid., p. 98.
25 J. Talboys Wheeler, *Early Travels in India: Reprints of Rare and Curious Narratives of Old Travellers in India, in the Sixteenth and Seventeenth Centuries*, London: Deep Publications (repr.), 1864, 1974, p. 18.
26 Ibid., p. 36.
27 William Foster, *Early Travels in India, 1583–1619*, London: Oxford University Press, p. 244.
28 Prasad, op.cit., p. 186.
29 'Weighty presence' where the Mughal emperors were concerned probably had more than one meaning.
30 Wheeler, op.cit., p. 37.
31 An early 16th-century English factor at Surat, who also travelled to Agra.
32 Ibid. This refers to Jahangir, not Akbar.
33 Arthur Coke Burnell and Pieter Anton Tiele (tr. and ed.), *The Voyage of John Huyghen van Linschoten to the East Indies*, 2 Vols., London: Hakluyt Society, 1885; Asian Educational Services Reprint, 1988, Introduction, p. xl. Linschoten's work seems to made publishing history of a sort for it was translated into English and German in 1598, two Latin translations were made in 1599 and a French one in 1610. The French and the original Dutch version were reprinted more than once.
34 Ibid., Vol. 1, p. 28.
35 Ibid., p. 29.
36 Ibid., p. 64.
37 Ibid., p. 101.
38 Venice was still *the* city state for all trading ventures.

4   Defining the east

In Europe, the beginning of the 17th century saw the sharpening of national identities, often in competition with other nations. Such competition could be expressed both directly and indirectly: the former through wars and the latter through markets. Increasingly, access to markets began to be not just a matter of individual merchants making a fortune, but also an issue of national prestige. The 17th century therefore saw official, state-level negotiations for trade concessions by the newer entrants into Asian waters, the English and the Dutch. New kinds of travel writing ensued – some official, some semi-official, and many increasingly judgemental. It is in these accounts that many of the stereotypes outlined earlier become much more firmly grounded. The number of travellers who came on official or semi-official work, or accompanied those who were on official work, increased tremendously. Some did still travel for the pleasure of travel alone, but they were very few in number, and can be seen only in the first half of the 17th century. Pietro della Valle is perhaps the best example of this kind of traveller; and for official, we have Sir Thomas Roe, Captain William Hawkins, Francisco Pelsaert, and many more, while semi-official travellers are perhaps best represented by Edward Terry and Thomas Herbert.

Pietro della Valle,[1] an Italian, came to India in 1623 and stayed till November 1624. As aforesaid, he apparently travelled for the pleasure of travel itself. He was a linguist of some note, for he spoke and wrote Turkish, Persian, and Arabic, all languages which were useful in India as well. He travelled extensively in Turkey, Persia, and India. In India, he restricted himself to the west coast and the Arabian sea, neither travelling inland, nor beyond India, into southeast Asia. He of course remarked on the extent of trade, describing the caravans carrying goods overland to the ports for export. Unlike earlier travellers, his concern was with the customs that he observed and not physical features or skin colour. For instance, he remarked on the number of people who were entering a "Temple of the Mahometans" in Cambay, "not onely Mahometans but likewise Gentiles."[2] He said that flowers and rice were given as offerings, and that flowers were sold at the entrance, but noted also that this was "rather a Custom of the Gentiles than Mahometans; and the Gentiles being more numerous and ancient in

Cambaia, 'tis no wonder that some Rite of theirs hath adher'd to the Mahometans."[3] He apparently tried to get some information about the religious practices, but was unable to do so, because those Indians he talked to were all "Factors or Merchants, and consequently unlearned . . . are not intelligible saving in buying and selling."[4] Unlike other travellers, he realised that the forms of ritual did not constitute the religion itself, believing that there was a deeper philosophy to which outsiders did not have access. Here, perhaps for the first time, we get proof of the multiple languages, the gaps that would result through not knowing the local languages, and so, of the need for many interlocutors.

In the 13th century, Rubruquis had remarked on the instruments of music used by the Mongols, saying that they had many musical instruments not known to Europeans. In the 17th century, della Valle said that the Indian instruments consisted of "Drums, Bells ty'd to the Arms, and the like, all of great noise".[5] Rubruquis had made no comment on the music itself, but della Valle said that the music was "too full of noise", and so was more "distasteful then pleasing" to him. Here again, there is no attempt to compare Indian systems of music to those he was more familiar with, all he was remarking on was his own reaction to the music. In fact, at a later place, he pointed out that custom and habit were of prime importance to "endear things to the eye, and make that fancy'd and esteem'd by some, which others, through want of custom, dislike, or value not".[6] He was even rather contemptuous of those who regarded the 'unusual' as 'unlawful', only because it was practised by Indians and not by Europeans.[7]

Something that is noticeable in the travel narratives from the 16th century onwards is that some information was always provided on the history of India. Barbosa at the beginning of the 16th century had given some details about the Sultanates of Gujarat and Bijapur. Fitch had described the establishment of the Mughal empire in north India, as had Linschoten. However, Linschoten had focussed more on south India. Della Valle too gave the same details, but like Linschoten earlier, concentrated more on the south than the north. Both were aware of the earlier prosperity of the Vijayanagar empire and its current state of decline. Thus, this loss of power and prosperity, as well as the conflicts between Vijayanagar and Deccani sultanates, was given in a fair amount of detail. But it should be remembered that history was a secondary concern, and was provided only for their readers, to give them a sense of the country and its kings. Names and places were on the whole unfamiliar, but as travel accounts became more widely read, there was an increasing familiarity with the more important dynasties of India. So, there were accounts, particularly about wars, but the focus was more often on the pomp and ceremony surrounding the courts and persons of the kings, rather than on political history.

If Pietro della Valle's writing was characterised by a certain tolerance, the same cannot be said for all other travellers of the time. The contrasts in attitudes can perhaps be seen most clearly in the writings of Thomas Herbert, Sir Thomas Roe, and Edward Terry.

Thomas Herbert travelled to the east early in the 17th century. The notion of difference began for him as soon as they sailed beyond the Canary Islands, because, as he said, they had then crossed the Tropic of Cancer. This crossing was marked by a sudden change in weather which became "incertaine and variable . . .; now blowing fresh and faire and forthwith storming outragiously, in one houres space the wind veering about every point of the compass".[8] The seas were no less strange, for they had all kinds of strange fish, including sharks. Stranger still, these sharks were always preceded by what he called 'pilot fish' that "scuds to and fro to bring intelligence".[9] Can we see in this yet another attempt to locate something familiar in an unfamiliar world? The 'pilot' boats guiding the larger ships to a safe harbour were already known, and perhaps it is this that Herbert is evoking.

If wind and water were so strange, then the lands surrounding these waters could be no less. The strangeness of course began the minute one sailed into African waters. Thus, Africa was first of all distinguished by a great many strangely named, countries – 'Monomotapa', 'Benomotapa' and 'Caffaria' – and worse still "full of wretched black skin'd wretches; rich in earth but miserable in demonomy."[10] Ethiopia was not strangely named but was strangely inhabited, for the people had no houses and lived only in caves. Strangest of all was that "the name of wife or brother [was] unknowne among these incestuous Troglodites."[11] Herbert's account includes in the list of all these oddities the banana, which, he told his readers, was a fruit with many good uses, but was to be peeled before being eaten. Statements such as this are not to be seen in earlier accounts.

It is noticeable that such attitudes were conspicuous by their absence when he discussed India. Herbert went into considerable detail about the different kinds of people, and while he did remark on the 'crafty, cowardly' nature of the Indian Muslims, he was quite admiring of the merchants and their ability. India was remarkable for its range of commercial activity and for the knowledge systems and the habits; for example, unlike in Africa, monogamy was the standard practice except among the kings. Indians may not have been Christian, but did have a clearly defined religious system, which he castigated as being idolatry, but which was an organised religion nonetheless. Where Christianity had ten commandments, he said that the Baniyas had eight, and this was their moral law which everyone had to observe or be exiled from the community. Perhaps most important, the Indians were clean, for they bathed twice every day whether they were dirty or not![12]

With Sir Thomas Roe and Edward Terry, we get both, an addition to such attitudes, and a fresh dimension to the descriptions, particularly of India. One feature that continues to stand out clearly in most of these writings is the centrality of India to the narratives – as land of fabulous wealth, of course, for the cornucopia of produce was only just beginning to be explored, but also as strange and exotic. The strangeness increasingly lay not in the skin colour, or in the lack of civilisation as defined by comparison with Africa or the countries to the east, like Burma and Pegu, but in the people themselves, and in their customs and practices. Most of all, the difference was discernible in the rulers.

In Sir Thomas Roe's narrative, the focus shifts to North India, and to English trade, but through official channels. Roe was the designated Ambassador of King James I to the court of the Emperor Jahangir. He was sent to negotiate with the Emperor on behalf of the English Crown to get concessions for trade for the English Company that had newly arrived in India. Roe was not the first ambassador, for Captain William Hawkins[13] had been sent in 1608 by King James I to the same court. William Hawkins was welcomed quite cordially and was given concessions, but these were not translated into ground reality, and so the English factors at Surat still had a great deal of trouble in carrying out their trade. King James I therefore decided to send out yet another mission, this time under Sir Thomas Roe who arrived in India in 1611. Roe made his way to Agra and stayed at the Emperor's court for almost the entire time that he spent in India. He was both conscious of the dignity of his own position and that of the nation he represented, and of the need to make sure that he did not antagonise the Emperor or his family and nobles, so that the concessions being asked for would not be refused. His was therefore much more of a tightrope act than the earlier travellers, for they did not have an official position to uphold.

Roe began his description of India with his meeting with Sultan Parvez, Emperor Jahangir's second son at Burhanpur. Knowing that the custom was to go with presents, and because "there was some purpose of erecting a factory in the town" he made a formal call on the prince.

> [A]t the outward court were about one hundred horsemen armed, being gentlemen that attend the Prince . . .: in the inner Court he sate high in a Gallery that went round, with a Canopy over him, and a Carpet before him, in great, but barbarous State.[14]

Roe's work is entirely concerned with court politics and procedure. He described the durbar, the daily routine of the king, the presents given to the king, and other such matters. It would perhaps not be wrong to treat his work as a court chronicle, not exactly in the same style as the Persian chronicles, but basically concerned with the same things. Both kinds of chroniclers were, in a sense, dependent on the king for their livelihood, the difference lay only in the areas of livelihood. They were, therefore, at the mercy of the king and his court, for the favour of the king was of prime importance. The difference, of course, lay in the fact that Roe was an outsider, and so, while taking note of the factions and court politics, he was not actually part of those politics. Still, he needed to understand them, to get what he wanted. Obviously, as he was associated with the court, he came into frequent contact with the royal family. Thus, his account provides considerable information about the princes, their powers, prowess, and ambitions. As the English company was at this time primarily occupied in trade in Surat and Gujarat, and from there into the Deccan, he was most concerned with Prince Khurram, the Viceroy of the Deccan. Both he and Peter Mundy (one of the factors of the English Company, who was based at Surat) mention the rebellion of Khurram in their accounts.

It is with Roe that, for the first time, we start getting a sense of moving away from acceptance of difference to the gradual emergence of a sense of superiority. He was the first to compare the durbar with a theatre – "the King in his Gallery; the great men lifted on a Stage, as Actors; the Vulgar below gazing on."[15] He met the Emperor fairly frequently and was questioned in detail about the European style of painting. He was also asked to provide a painter who could demonstrate that style, which, apparently, he was unable to do. However, he presented the Emperor with a painting, and a few weeks later, was shown two paintings, and asked to identify the original that he had given. He was unable to identify it, and his account has specific mention of the ability of the Indian painters to duplicate that which was given to them – something that finds an echo in the 19th century, when it was said that the Indian worker had no originality but could make perfect copies of anything he was given.

His stay at the royal court was one which seems to have been rather frustrating. What emerges in his writing is a feeling that the word of the Emperor was not really to be trusted, something which became rather more common later – at one place, he said that he had spent seven months getting promises "from weeke to weeke, from day to day, and no exception", but had received nothing in writing. Factory records of the late 17th and early 18th century echo the sentiment, if not the words.

He provided, naturally, a great many more details about the visible luxury of the court, as seen in the clothes and jewellery that the Emperor wore – a "sword and buckler, sett all over with great Diamonds and Rubies . . ., on one side hung a Rubie unset, as bigge as a Walnut; on the other side a Diamond as great, in the middle an Emerald like a heart, much bigger. His Shash was wreathed about with a chaine of great Pearle, Rubies and Diamonds."[16] This visible display of wealth was clearly something totally unfamiliar to Roe, even though, as Ambassador of the King, he had been part of the English court scene as well and can therefore be assumed to be reasonably familiar with the trappings of royalty. Here was a visible difference between 'east' and 'west' – the words themselves are not used, but the sense of a mental and material distance between the two begins to be much clearer.

Edward Terry was the chaplain who accompanied Sir Thomas Roe, and according to his own claim lived "more than two years at the court of that mighty monarch the great Moghul".[17] As a chaplain, his main preoccupation was religion, and he was both censorious and judgemental. This attitude can be seen from the very beginning; in fact, from his description of the climate and people of Africa. The winds, he declared, were contrary and "within the space of one hour, all the 32 several winds . . . will blow".[18] This kind of variation he laid at the door of Satan who, he believed, ruled both land and people, declaring that Satan ruled over "the inhabitants on that main, the poor, ignorant, and most miserable negroes, born for sale, slavery, and slaughter".[19] The natives of the area near the Cape of Good Hope, he said, loved brass "for the rankness of its smell"[20] and he believed that given a choice between gold and brass they would choose brass. Their speech was even more uncivilised, seeming to him like "inarticulate noise, rather than language, like the clucking of hens or gabling of turkeys".[21] Following the trend that had already begun, Terry too commented on their physiology, and pointed out that they were not very tall, had flat noses, and black curly hair. On the other hand, he was the first to remark that if they were given "the accommodations we enjoy," they would welcome the change.[22]

A sense of the differences between India and Africa also come out in his account. Thus, when he described the island of 'Mohelia', he said that it was

> very pleasant, full of trees, and exceeding fruitful, abounding in beeves, kids, poultries of divers kinds, rice, sugar-canes, plantens . . . oranges, cocoa-nuts, . . .; of all which we had sufficient to relieve our whole company, for little quantities of white paper, glass beads, low-pric'd looking glasses, and cheap knives; for instance, we bought as many good oranges as would fill a hat for a quarter of a sheet of white writing paper, and so in proportion all other provisions.[23]

Implied in such statements was the contrast between this and the sophisticated commercial transactions that took place in India.

Accuracy of geographical knowledge was something that Terry emphasised. So, along with his details about the length and the breadth of India he took care to point out

> a great error in geographers . . . who . . . make East-India and China near neighbours, when so many large countries are interposed betwixt them; which great distance may appear by the long travel of the Indian merchants, who are usually (they going and returning all the way by land) in their journey and return, . . . two full years from Agra to China.[24]

He is the only traveller to point to the continued trade contacts between India and China.

The wealth of India was a recurring theme in his narrative. Saying that the country "so much abounds in all necessaries for the use and service of man, to feed, and cloath, and enrich him, as that it is able to subsist and flourish of itself, without the least help from any neighbour – prince or nation,"[25] he also laid the basis for yet another recurring theme of later writings, that the people of 'the east' were lazier because they got what they needed for their subsistence without having to work hard (unlike the people of the west).[26] In addition to the natural produce was the expertise of Indians in craft; they not only had a phenomenal range of cotton and silk cloth, but were also experts in woodwork, ivory work and cutting precious stones. His praise was always tempered though. And so, he said that "the natives of that monarchy are the best apes for imitation in the world, so full of ingenuity, that they will make any new thing by pattern, how hard soever it seem to be done."[27]

Terry was very clear that Indians had a great many things "to make their lives more comfortable". The rulers also did their bit to make life better, at least for themselves, if not for the populace as a whole. For them, one part of this comfort lay in the landscaped Mughal gardens "planted with fruitfull Trees and delightfull Flowers . . . [with] pleasant Fountaynes to bathe in". Once again, though, there is a caveat – perhaps in keeping with the Biblical belief of the serpent in Eden, there were a great many dangers just outside these planned spaces. These were

> first many harmful beasts of prey, as lions, tigers, wolves, jackals, with others; those jackals seem to be wild dogs, who in great companies run up and down in the silent night. . . . Those most ravenous creatures will not suffer a man to rest quietly in his grave. . . . In their rivers are many crocodiles, and on the land, not a few overgrown snakes, with other venomous and pernicious creatures. In our houses there we often see lizards, shaped like unto crocodiles. . . . There are many scorpions to be seen, which are oftentimes felt, which creep into their houses, especially in that time of the rains, whose stinging is most sensible and deadly.[28]

Familiarity for him lay in Europe, and therefore in the presence of European ships. He talked about a Dutch ship on its way to Bantam that they encountered at the Cape of Good Hope, and later, a Portuguese carrack near Madagascar which was on its way to Goa (and which the English attacked). All these places were mapped and were known. Thus, the familiar was located through the exercise of mapping and trading. Even if familiarity existed, the fact remained that these were strange lands. The strangeness was to be seen everywhere, and thus one can see in the narratives a sense of distance between those observing the lands, and the lands and peoples that they were observing.

A slightly later account is that of Peter Mundy, whose is a different kind of official narrative. Roe had come in as ambassador and so was involved at court and higher levels; Mundy was an employee of the East India Company and so directly concerned with the nitty-gritty of commercial transactions and identification of products that could be sent to England on the company's account. His can, perhaps, be seen as among the earliest English accounts that was primarily commercial in purpose. Not surprisingly, his first concern was with the transport of goods. He described the caravans and took particular note of the way in which guard was kept over the caravan itself at night, which he described as being by the "Continuall beatinge of a great Kettle Drumme . . ., and once in a quarter or halfe an hower one or other cryes, Covardare, when all the rest of the people answer with a shout Covardare [*khabardar*], which is as much to say as take heed."[29] That this manner of watching was the norm later as well is clear from Bernier's account of the guards who were hired by noblemen to keep a watch on their camps. The same practice he saw at the royal camp also, where guards were "posted round the whole army at every five hundred paces, who kindle fires and cry out Kaberdar."[30]

Mundy also went into details about the method of purchase of cloth and the important centres of cloth manufacture. He was also among the earliest to give the names of varieties of cloth. As his was the time that the East India Company was trying to purchase indigo, he also had considerable information about indigo manufacture. In 1634, when Mundy returned to England and submitted his accounts to the Company for auditing, it was stated that he "had brought home his whole estate in indico and Callicoes."[31] I have pointed out elsewhere[32] that Mundy's account has been extensively used for the study of the economic history of India of the 17th century, but as a traveller whose narrative was read by lay people also in England, it added to the already circulating stories about India's wealth and the contrasts within India, in addition to the existing knowledge of the differences between India and England. So, it underlined the emerging perception about the basic difference of east and west.

Mundy, Terry, and della Valle were among the earliest to talk about the caste system – not in the way that Varthema did where details were given only about Malabar, but about the system as a whole – as well as the rituals that were followed. For Mundy and della Valle, the rituals were to be commented on; for Terry they were to be castigated.

With Mundy, there is still a tolerance visible – or rather, an equal contempt of both Indian and European superstitions. For example, he reported one of the stories about the Son river, which he crossed on his way back from Patna to Agra. He was told that the river was so called because in its bed lay the 'Paros' – the *parasmani* – which he said was the equivalent of the western philosopher's stone, believed to turn any metal that touched it into gold. The river Son was the river of gold. Mundy was equally contemptuous of Indian and European beliefs because he said that despite every effort made, the stone could not be found, "noe more then wee in Europe can doe with all our studdies."[33]

Mundy was also the first of the travellers to talk about the way in which time was measured in India. Calculation was in *pahars* and the day was divided into eight pahars: "4 in the day and 4 in the night, whether longe or shorte". A pahar was subdivided into *gharis*, each ghari consisting of "22½ minutes of tyme" and eight gharis made one pahar.

> Some measure it by a little brasse dish with a hole att bottome, which vessell of water, and when it sincketh by the water that commeth in att the little hole aforesaid, then it is one gree [ghari], which they give to

understand by strikeing on a great Copper plate, with a wooden hammer in stead of a Bell, soe many grees as it is.[34]

Another contemporary traveller, representing another European company, was the Dutchman Francisco Pelsaert. Pelsaert came to India in 1620 and was sent to Agra where he remained until 1627. He was the representative of the Dutch at Jahangir's court and therefore, like Roe, he was greatly concerned with the court and the court politics. While he did not talk of the theatricality of the court, he was possibly the first to clearly state the extent of the control that Nur Jahan had over Jahangir. His description of the administration of the country began by stating that "Jahangir, disregarding his own person and position, has surrendered himself to a crafty wife of humble lineage. . . . [The] King's orders or grants of appointments etc., are not certainties, being of no value until they have been approved by the Queen."[35] He went on to say that nothing was permanent,

> even the noble buildings – gardens, tombs, or palaces, which, in and near every city, one cannot contemplate because of their ruined state. For in this they are to be despised above all the laziest nations of the world, because they build them with so many hundreds of thousands, and yet keep them in repair only so long as the owners live and have the means.[36]

He was also the first to talk about the autocratic government, for he said that while there were books of laws, the laws were hardly observed "until avarice has had its share."[37]

Pelsaert said that there were only three classes of people, the rich, the poor, and the merchants. There was a tremendous contrast between the "manner of life of the rich in their great superfluity and absolute power, and the utter subjection and poverty of the common people".[38] Wages for the workers were extremely low, and exploitation by the upper classes made matters worse, for, according to Pelsaert, when any work was done for a nobleman, the workers were often not paid at all and forced to work. The biggest marker of poverty, for him, was that most people did not eat meat. Like Terry, he was quite critical of the religious practices of both Hindus and Muslims. As a Protestant, he often compared Muslim practices or beliefs with the Catholics, so for example, he said that Muslims had "among them as many *pirs*, or prophets, as the papists have saints" and perhaps the only saving grace for the Muslims was that no images were made of these saints.[39] Hinduism, he declared, could not be explained or described for it had "no foundation beyond elaborate poetic fables", but had a lot of rituals which they were very strict about observing. Like Terry, he too remarked on the importance given to bathing.[40]

It is with Pelsaert that we start to find many of the statements that became stereotypical of India later. As said earlier, he was the first to talk of Nur

60   Defining the east

Jahan's influence; something that found its way into later history writing as the 'Nur Jahan Junta'. Licentiousness of particularly the upper classes was another recurring theme. Both men and women drank, and he said that drinking had "become very fashionable in the last few years".[41] Slave girls were of course at the service of their masters and, perhaps following Jahangir's example, all nobles kept large harems. While houses of the rich were opulent, most of the people lived in mud houses with thatched roofs and very little furniture, and in winter suffered because of lack of clothing. Here are all the features that we find repeated over and over again in the 19th-century writings – of poverty, of exploitation, of superstition, and of loose morals.

Pelsaert's view was perhaps a rather extreme one for his time, but it was not entirely unusual. For example, earlier travellers like Barbosa had remarked that there were very few large houses to be seen even in the more important ports and the norm was small, thatched houses. Varthema had talked of the fascination that eastern women had for his white skin, and an early 17th-century traveller, Nicholas Whittington, provided a long description of how a man had found his way into a harem, escorted by a eunuch. Whittington and his contemporaries had in addition talked of Jahangir's harem consisting of 300 women.[42]

Subsequent narratives seem to pick up Pelsaert's comments and often extend them. Thus, later writings such as those of Dr. John Fryer tend to very consciously point to the difference between 'us' and 'them'. The 'us' was usually all Europeans and the 'them' the Indians or any other Asians. But when there were no Asians in the equations, the 'them' could be the English, or the Dutch or the French depending on who was writing; thus, Dutch accounts talk of the inequities of the Portuguese, the English of the problems caused by the Dutch to their trade, or, a little later, of the potential for trouble because of the proximity of the French.

John Fryer was the second of the medical doctors to come to India, the first being Francois Bernier. Fryer came to India in 1672,[43] at a time when the East India Company was quite well established. The Mughal Empire was still visibly flourishing, but there were also newer entrants on the political scene, one of whom was Shivaji. As the British traded, or wanted to trade, in the areas controlled by Shivaji, much of Fryer's account is devoted to Maratha-British relations. He stated that he had originally not planned to write an account as there had been too many travellers who had already published their works, but later changed his mind because of the length of his stay in India as a result of which he decided to "offer some Novelties, either passed over by them, or else not so thoroughly observed."[44]

As had become the norm in travel accounts of the 17th century, Fryer too began his narrative with the departure from England and with details about the voyage to the east. All the travellers of this century have certain common themes about the voyage – the storms at sea, the variable winds and the sharks. In a sense the water itself seems to have become the first marker of difference. Most also mentioned the different kinds of birds that were to be found on the two coasts of Africa, and Fryer made particular mention of the Albatross, remarkable "in that they have great Bodies, yet not proportionable to their Wings which mete out twice their length."[45]

Clear from Fryer's narrative is first of all the familiarity with the route to the east. Therefore, the markers of the route no longer needed to be described in detail, only named. So, for example, where earlier accounts like those of Mundy had gone into detail about the problems of navigation because of currents and winds near Madagascar, in Fryer we get a very matter-of-fact statement about the easier passage being between Madagascar and the mainland, rather than around the island. Of far greater interest to him was that Madagascar was "reckoned one of the four biggest islands in the world" the others being Sumatra, Java, and Britain.[46] By the end of the 17th century, and in the 18th century, the same passage once again began to be defined as dangerous, but now because of pirates.

The other dimension of familiarity of the route was the possibility of acquiring information about India in advance. For example, near the Cape of Good Hope they came across two ships which he said were "English built". They boarded the first of the two ships, which was the lead ship of a convoy of five ships on its return journey from Bantam, and got some information about the state of affairs, local as well as Company, at the time of departure of the ships. However, the convoy had been dispersed because of tempests. Statements about ships dispersing because of tempests are another recurring theme in the writing from the 17th century onwards. What was relevant to Fryer and the ships moving towards India was that the French had arrived on the Coromandel coast, where Fryer was headed, had "worsted Flemmings in India, taken and demolished a fort on the island Ceylon; and that they had beat the Moors out of St. Thomas."[47]

Fryer too picked up a theme from travellers like Linschoten – that of skin colour. The people of the island of St. Jago (off the coast of Africa) were described as "of a comely Black, their Hair frizled. Tall of stature, cunning and Thievish: they staring one in the Face, and in the mean time cut a Knot from the Shoulder or steal an Handkerchief out of the Pocket."[48] In his account, for the first time, we find mention of attempts to imitate the Europeans; he says that these people spoke Portuguese, and tried their best to imitate the Portuguese style of dress. If they managed to wear something in the Portuguese style, they looked "as big as the greatest Don in Portugal".[49] He then described the people of Madagascar as being a little less black, "as well Limb'd, and as well Featur'd; neither so tall, nor so proud as them, but more honest: Whether out of fear of Punishment, or natural Integrity, may be left to conjecture."[50] On arrival at Masulipatam, they were met by local boatmen, who "were of a Sun-burnt Black, with long black Hair, tied up in a Clout of Calicut Lawn, girt about the Middle with a Sash, in their Ears Rings of Gold."[51] His descriptions are different from those of the beginning of the century, not in what they described, but in the way they described. So, where Linschoten stopped with skin colour, Fryer went on into speculation about their character. While there is no obvious link being made yet between skin colour and morality, one can see the beginnings of a rather more judgemental attitude.

This attitude is particularly visible when Fryer described the women and the religion. Muslim women were of course veiled, but this, he said, was because Muslim men were

> by Nature plagued with Jealousy, cloistring their Wives up, and sequestring them the sight of any besides the Capon that watches them. When they go abroad, they are carried in close Palenkeens, which if a Man offer to unveil it is present death; the meanest of them not permitting their Women to stir out uncovered.[52]

Hindu women were permitted more freedom, in that they did not have to wear the veil, but the words he used seem to imply the exact opposite. So, he says "women are manacled with Chains of Silver (or Fetters rather) and hung with Ear-rings of Gold and Jewels, their Noses stretched with weighty Jewels, on their Toes rings of Gold".[53]

Religion and rituals were also approached with a highly censorious attitude. He remarked on ceremonies being "usher'd in with Tumult; in the middle of them were carried their Gods in State, garnished with the Riches of the Orient; they were cut in horrid shapes".[54] He was also critical of the knowledge systems, and, as a doctor, said that Indians had no knowledge of "Physical" (medicine), anatomy, surgery or pharmacy – so, "every one ventures and every one suffers."[55] They were definitely adept with mathematics, for they were able to "arithmetic the nicest Fractions without the help of Pen or Ink; much given to Traffick, and intelligent in the way of Merchandize, if not fraudulent".[56] They also had mastery over certain aspects of technology, particularly those concerned with the manufacture and dyeing of cloth. Here, for the first time, one can see the basis of a common refrain of a later period, that Indians had only technology, not the scientific basis of technology.

Unlike Pelsaert, he was quite admiring of houses, especially in Masulipatam.[57] Masulipatam, he said, was a city with broad streets, lined with "high and lofty Buildings, the Materials wood and Plaister, beautified without with folding Windows, made of Wood, and lattised with Rattans, entring into Balconies shaded by large Sheds covered with Tiles".[58] Poorer houses were mud and thatch. The difference between the descriptions of Masulipatnam and other towns in India and that of Johanna town on the island of the same name off the coast of Africa is marked. Johanna, he said, was "Three quarters of a Mile in length, and may contain Two hundred Houses; their Streets being no broader than our Allies".[59] Masulipatnam had a wooden bridge to the north-east of the town that was half a mile long and a mile long one on the north-west of the town.

Despite the increase in knowledge that comes out so clearly in Fryer, some older stories still continued. For example, a Portuguese tradition about the martyrdom of St. Thomas said that those responsible for his murder were cursed by God with an illness. Fryer, echoing this story, said that near St. Thomas mount, near Chennai, lived "a Cast of People, one of whose Legs are as big as an Elephant's; which gives occasion for the divulging it to be a Judgement on them, as the Generation of Assassins and Murtherers of the Blessed Apostle St. Thomas."[60]

A slightly earlier traveller was the Frenchman Abbé Carré, a French priest who travelled to India via Syria, Persia, and the Persian Gulf, and spent the years between 1672 and 1674 in these travels.[61] In India, he travelled from Surat by sea to Chennai, on the other side of the peninsula, and then back to Bombay (again by sea) before retracing his route back to France. He was a traveller not for personal profit or for the French Company, but was given orders by the King of France to examine the functioning of the French East India Company, and submit reports on them to the King and his minister, Colbert.[62] The dedication at the beginning of his work stated that it would "show clearly the most hidden and secret things that [had] occurred in the administration of [the French Company's] trade in these distant Eastern lands," as well as the "methods, the feelings, and the enterprises of those you have administered your affairs in these countries."[63] He followed the older route, partly overland and then by sea, for he went first to Italy, and then across the Mediterranean, stopping at Cyprus before disembarking at Alexandretta. Thereafter, he travelled overland to Aleppo, from where he travelled, again overland, to Baghdad, from there to Basra and Kung. On the overland route, he particularly remarked on the hospitality that he received from the Arabs, which he said was the norm even though they seemed

> so far away from the courtesies and civilities of other nations that one is apt to believe them ignorant of good manners. . . . All travellers, whether Arabs or strangers, when passing by Arab towns, villages or encampments, are ordinarily lodged in the house or tent of the Sheikh, or with one of the principal men, as freely as we go to hotels in France. . . . They shame most of our rich Christians in Europe, who often refuse a piece of bread to poor pilgrims.[64]

The overland route continued to be well used for trade and pilgrimage, and by the East India Companies, to send letters which could not go by sea because of the change of season.

Having reached Basra, he managed to get passage on one of the ships of the Portuguese fleet that was to leave for Goa. Approaching the Indian coast, he was given the option of landing at the Portuguese possession of Diu, which he accepted, believing that it would be easier to reach Surat overland from Diu than from Goa.

The continued involvement of Asians in the trade of Asia and the value of that trade is also clear from his account. Carré had met the "great caravan from Baghdad" on his journey across the desert. It had more than "2,000 loads of valuable goods from Persia, India and all the East for Aleppo",[65] but the statement does not in any way indicate that such a rich caravan was particularly out of the ordinary. Further proof of the wealth of trade can also be seen in his description of an Armenian merchant's ship from Surat that he saw at the mouth of the Persian Gulf. This particular ship was commanded by an Englishman and was one of four ships owned by the merchant. Carré said that "their yearly trade with all the oriental kingdoms brought him more revenue than he would have got from the best estate" in France. When he reached India, he met other merchants who had quite as large and as profitable a trade across the Bay of Bengal and the Arabian Sea.

Like Mundy, he too remarked on India's religion, but from a very different perspective. He stated that the Hindus had "suffered an intense persecution from the Mughal, who (as a zealous follower of Muhammadan law) has wished to destroy all their pagodas and idols."[66] A certain amount of persecution had been stopped by the payment of money, but Carré was very clear that the problems had been instigated by the Muslims, who believed that their religion was "so superior to other religions that it ennobles anybody who follows it, because of the privileges and the authority they imagine it confers over those of other nations, whom they hold in contempt."[67] Carré was the first of the travellers to make such categorical statements about the Muslims, and unlike others, had very little to say about Hindu practices and beliefs. Where other travellers saw in those practices much to remark on, he apparently took for granted that there were differences. Where other travellers almost invariably remarked on the size of the harems of the kings, Carré stated that the king of Bijapur had 1,400 women in his harem, but went on to say that "as in Europe the magnificence of our Christian princes is shown by a splendid stable of the finest horses from all over the world, so these Eastern princes show their power and grandeur by their seraglios, where they have women brought from every foreign kingdom."[68] He did go on to compare the women in such harems to sheep, and to say that the kings thought nothing of presenting one of the women to a noble as a special mark of favour – and to add that the women enjoyed the change, rather than objecting to it! Judgemental attitudes were mainly reserved for that with which he was more familiar – Christians and Muslims. So, where on the one hand he talked of the Muslims believing that their religion was superior to all others, on the other he criticised the Portuguese Christians, complaining of their "want of devotion".[69] He was also very indignant at the "injustices and bad treatment inflicted by them on all European ecclesiastics when they come to the East."[70]

Carré described both, the problems of the French company, and the political troubles in the area, in great detail. Surat had been raided by Shivaji a few years before Carré's arrival in India, and his power was definitely in the ascendant. Further south, in the sultanate of Bijapur, there was trouble because of the death of the Sultan and the succession issues that had come up since. In accordance with his instruction, he made careful note of the functioning of the Company, the problems that it was likely to face within India, and the problems that had cropped up because of internal rivalries. He was concerned with competition, and the failure of France to hold her own in this competition. Thus, descriptions had to focus not on products, which were already well known, but on practices of Europeans, their weaknesses and strengths, and on the problems that were likely to come up vis-à-vis both Europeans and Indian rulers.

India and the east were still the fabulously wealthy lands. But the reverse of the cornucopia was that India was also beginning to be seen as the land into which gold vanished. Carré did not talk about the hoarding tendencies of the Asian merchants in general and Indian merchants in particular, but this became a recurring theme in colonial historiography of the 19th century, which emphasised the inability of Indians to invest in order to generate wealth.

It should perhaps be pointed out that while the east was increasingly being fixed from Turkey eastwards, there were still some older definitions of the east that prevailed, which located the east in Europe itself. This can be seen in one account of the middle of the 17th century, that of Guy Miège.[71] He was part of the diplomatic mission sent by Charles II to Russia, Sweden, and Denmark in 1663 and 1664 and while Miège never travelled further east than Moscow, he definitely believed he was in the east there.

The beginning of Miège's narrative is very similar to descriptions of voyages to the east: voyages began with storms, a few days of stormy weather were invariably followed by fair winds and fair weather when the travellers could see different kinds of fish, including whales (as against sharks in the African and Asian waters). The voyage to Archangel was of course shorter and so the journey was completed in a month or a little over, obviously very different from the journey eastwards. Miège was clear that the empire of 'Muscovie' was in Europe and was the greatest in that continent, but it was still very different from the Europe that Miège was familiar with. The first difference lay in the weather, where there were extremes of heat and cold. His description of the clouds of wasps and flies that infested the country in summer is very similar to the descriptions provided of mosquitoes in India. Muscovy, he said, produced a great many goods and had an abundance of birds of different kinds which could also be eaten. There were also any number of fruits. The people were of great "Wit, Cunning, and Dexterity". They were physically robust, but were prone to laziness and had a great "Antipathy to all kind of labour. It must be either force or necessity that compels them thereunto, they often preferring a bastinado or whipping before an honest but painful imployment."[72] He went on to say that they were "very good Slaves, but would make the worst Free-men in the World."[73] All this was distinctly different from Europe, but what made it most like the east was the form of monarchy, which was "Despotical and Absolute in so much as the Tzar being lord and master (as it were) over all his Subjects, disposeth uncontroulably of their lives and estates, as he thinks good."[74] At almost

66 *Defining the east*

the same time, Francois Bernier in his description of India talked about the king owning all the land and made specific mention of the system of escheat.

Miège, though, was the exception, not the rule. He followed the older tradition of the Friars where once beyond the Caspian Sea or near the Volga they had entered the East. General understanding now did locate the east from the eastern shores of the Mediterranean onwards. Byzantium had already been perceived as the east; and after 1453, with the takeover of Constantinople by the Ottomans, the former Byzantium empire was clearly 'east'. Increasingly, the east was becoming fixed, different, but still problematic. The problems were now less of potential danger through warfare and more of differences in social and political structures.

Notes

1 Edward Grey (ed.), *The Travels of Pietro Della Valle in India*, 2 Vols., London: Hakluyt Society, 1892; Asian Educational Services Reprint, 1991.
2 Ibid., Vol. 1, p. 69.
3 Ibid.
4 Ibid., p. 72.
5 Ibid., p. 71.
6 Ibid., Vol. 2, pp. 195–196.
7 Ibid.
8 Thomas Herbert, *Some Years Travels into Africa and Asia the Great, Especially Describing the Famous Empires of Persia and Industant: As also Divers Other Kingdoms in the Orientall Indies, and Iles Adjacent*, London: Jacob Blome and Richard Bishop, 1638, p. 7.
9 Ibid.
10 Ibid., p. 9.
11 Ibid., p. 17. The word troglodytes had begun to be used in the middle of the 16th century and seems to have referred to people at a lower, because earlier, stage of civilisation.
12 Ibid., pp. 37–44.
13 The account of Captain William Hawkins has not been included in this work even though a lot of it fits in with the other narratives included here.
14 *Travels in India in the Seventeenth Century by Sir Thomas Roe and Dr. John Fryer: Reprinted from the "Calcutta Weekly Englishman"*, London: Turner and Co., 1873, Asian Educational Services Reprint, 1993, p. 17.
15 Ibid., p. 21.
16 Ibid., p. 73.
17 Edward Terry, *A Voyage to the East Indies*, Preface, London: J. Wilkie, S. Hayes, W. Cater and E. Easton, revised version 1655, p. iv.
18 Ibid., p. 6.
19 Ibid.
20 Ibid., p. 14.
21 Ibid., p. 16.
22 Ibid., p. 19. But he also provided examples to show that even when such 'charity' was shown to some of these people they ran away rather than take advantage of the benefits that they being given.
23 Ibid., pp. 50–51.
24 Ibid., p. 86.
25 Ibid., p. 87.

26 See Chapter 2, where Odoric seems to imply that, as fish came in on their own, no effort was required to catch them!
27 Ibid., pp. 127–129. This is an idea that was repeated in the 19th century when under colonialism it was declared that the Indian craftsman had no originality but could duplicate anything that was given to him.
28 Ibid., pp. 114–116.
29 Richard Carnac Temple (ed.), *The Travels of Peter Mundy, in Europe and Asia 1608–1667*, Vol. 2: *Travels in Asia 1628–1634*, London: Hakluyt Society, 1914, p. 43.
30 Archibald Constable (tr. and ed.), *Francois Bernier's Travels in Mogul Empire A.D. 1656–1666*, first published 1891, revised Vincent Smith, London: Oxford University Press, 1916; First Indian reprint, New Delhi: Oriental Books Reprint Corporation, 1983, p. 369.
31 Mundy, op.cit., p. 337.
32 Radhika Seshan, "Travellers' Tales: From Mandeville to Mundy", Radhika Seshan (ed.), *Convergences: Rethinking India's Past*, New Delhi: Primus Books, 2014, pp. 55–62.
33 Mundy, op.cit., p. 166.
34 Mundy, ibid., p. 169. Apparently, 18th-century and later writers who insisted that Indians had no measurement of time had not read Mundy.
35 William Harrison Moreland and Pieter Geyl (tr. and ed.), *Jahangir's India: The Remonstrantie of Francisco Pelsaert*, Cambridge: W. Heffer & Sons Ltd., 1925, Indian Edition, New Delhi: Idarah-I Adabiyat-I Delli, 1972, p. 50.
36 Ibid., p. 56.
37 Ibid., p. 57.
38 Ibid., p. 60.
39 Ibid., p. 69.
40 Ibid., p. 76.
41 Ibid., p. 69.
42 J. Talboys Wheeler, *Early Travels in India: Reprints of Rare and Curious Narratives of Old Travellers in India, in the Sixteenth and Seventeenth Centuries*, London, 1864; Indian Reprint, New Delhi: Deep Publications, 1974, pp. 18, 36, 72.
43 William Crooke (ed.), *A New Account of East India and Persia, Being Nine Years Travel, 1672–1681, by John Fryer*, London: Asian Educational Services Reprint, 1909, 1992, pp. 88–89.
44 *Travels in India*, op.cit., p. 5.
45 Ibid., p. 151. For Fryer, in this century, the myths of the albatross were either unknown or unimportant, for he did not report any of the superstitions regarding the albatross.
46 *Travels in India*, op.cit., p. 153.
47 Ibid.
48 Ibid., p. 45.
49 Ibid.
50 Ibid., pp. 64–65.
51 Ibid., p. 78.
52 Crooke, op.cit., pp. 88–89.
53 Ibid., p. 89.
54 John Fryer, *A New Account of East-India and Persia, in Eight Letters*, London: R. Chiswell, 1698.
55 Ibid., p. 286
56 Ibid., p. 90.
57 This was the chief port of the kingdom of Golconda, and occupied a position similar to that of Surat on the west coast.

58 Ibid., p. 80.
59 Fryer, op.cit., p. 161.
60 Crooke, op.cit., p. 116. The reference is probably to elephantiasis, a disease that was prevalent in this area until about twenty years ago.
61 Lady Fawcett and Charles Fawcett (tr. and ed.), *The Travels of the Abbé Carré in India and the Near East, 1672–1674*, 2 Vols., New Delhi: Asian Educational Services (reprint), 1990.
62 Ibid., Vol. 1, introduction, p. xiii.
63 Ibid., p. 1.
64 Fawcett (tr.) and Fawcett (ed.), op.cit., pp. 54–55.
65 Ibid., p. 59.
66 Ibid., pp. 139–140.
67 Ibid., p. 140.
68 Ibid., p. 247.
69 Ibid., p. 208.
70 Ibid., p. 211.
71 Guy Miège, *A Relation of Three Embassies from His Sacred Majestie Charles II to the Great Duke of Muscovie, the King of Sweden, and the King of Denmark: Performed by the Right Honorable the Earle of Carlisle in the Years 1663 & 1664*, London: John Starkey, 1669, accessed on Google Play, 3 October 2014.
72 Ibid., pp. 44–45.
73 Ibid., p. 49.
74 Ibid., p. 57.

5 Recasting the east

As a genre, travel writing acquired greater importance from the 16th century. Such writings could, as said earlier, allow the armchair traveller to experience vicariously all the dangers involved in going to strange parts of the globe, while sitting comfortably at home. In the process, these accounts could provide accurate information about the world, something that in the context of the Renaissance was becoming steadily more important. It was a window to the world, which could be opened or closed according to one's wishes, and could either influence one to go out and experience that world, or stay at home and revel in the familiar.

Travel however, did not begin with long-distance voyages to the east. For the English, it probably began with travel just across the Channel to Europe. Thus, we have what is perhaps the earliest category of travel writing in English: a series of 'Instructions to Travellers', which were regularly published through the 16th century.[1] These were not travelogues or guidebooks or travel accounts of the kind described earlier. They were essentially a series of essays which told travellers what they were to carry, and which places they were to go to in order to receive the best benefits of travel and then be able to return home with a 'complete education'. Implicit in this is a belief that travel was necessary to round out the person.

These instructions begin to die out by the first few decades of the 17th century. In the mid-18th century and the 19th century, after Napoleon's defeat, they were replaced by the diaries and reminiscences of the 'Grand Tour' that members of the English aristocracy undertook, so that the nobleman could 'see' the world and maybe come back confirmed in his belief that his own nation was the best. Those who went on the Grand Tour travelled with their own entourage, usually did not go into any of the more remote areas of the countries they visited and stayed in towns to mingle only with members of their own class. They did not need instructions on how or where to travel, for they already knew what to do and where to go. It was in the period between the decline of the instructions and the records of the Grand Tour that we have the kind of travel narratives which have been discussed in this volume.

Reminiscences and memoirs, while interesting in the way they show the mentality of the time, were rather different from the kinds of travel undertaken earlier. It has been argued that the accounts can also be seen as laying the groundwork for ethnographic material, which "provided a ground on which [to establish moral and cultural challenges] to the new spheres of discourse."[2] The kinds of travels undertaken from the 16th century are undoubtedly indicative of a new mindset that had begun to emerge. In that century, the English, after the Germans, were regarded as the greatest travellers amongst the nations. Such travel was initially in the form of pilgrimages. In 1434, for example, Henry VI granted 2,433 licenses to pilgrims wanting to visit the shrine of St. James of Compostella.[3] It was reported that "ships were every year loaded from different ports with cargoes of these deluded wanderers, who carried with them large sums of money to defray the expenses of their journey."[4] The earliest of the instructions to travellers, a work called *Informacon for Pylgrymes unto the Holy Lande*, was first published in 1498, the year Vasco da Gama reached India, republished in 1515, when Albuquerque had established Goa as his capital and then again in 1524, when the Portuguese cartaz[5] and monopoly system were well in place. The book provided fairly detailed instructions on where and when to board the ship (in England), which of the many ports that allowed access to the Holy Land was more suitable, and among other things, advised the pilgrim to carry at least two barrels of wine and enough provisions to supplement the food that would be provided both on board ship and at the various inns that he stayed in on the way. Obviously, the pilgrims being catered for were not poor or indigent, and probably belonged, if not to the upper classes, then at least to the reasonably wealthy ones. Some instructions also told the traveller to make sure that he was the first off the ship, for otherwise, he would not find a 'good' place in which to stay.

However, over a period of time, travel for its own sake rather than as a journey of pilgrimage started becoming more important. Increasingly, travel began to be affirmed as a way of broadening the mind. A great many Englishmen were sent out of England to the continent of Europe to study first-hand the systems existing in what were still regarded as the most civilised nations in the world, France and Italy. The new generation of travellers very often still belonged to the upper or wealthy classes, but now they were being prepared for a career in government, for any personal knowledge of the customs of the countries that they would be dealing with would be an advantage.

This new attitude started making its appearance in England during the time of Henry VIII. England, under his rule, was increasingly involved in the Continent, not so much from the point of view of political involvement, but as part of the intellectual ferment that was happening there. Henry VIII identified young scholars at Cambridge or at Oxford and sent them abroad to Italy or to France so that they could get better knowledge of the world. Some of those whom he sent later became ambassadors of the King. Travel was particularly important for those aspiring to positions in the government because it allowed them to learn 'modern languages'. In the 16th century, for instance, Francis Bacon, in his essay *On Travaille*, said that "Travel, in the younger sort is a part of education, in the elder, a part of experience."[6] He particularly pointed to the need to note 'shipping and navies' and 'houses and gardens of state and pleasure'. Latin had already begun to be replaced as the language of government and diplomacy by other languages, particularly French and Italian. Renaissance thought and philosophy too were expressed in the different vernacular languages and not in Latin. To keep abreast of these new dimensions of thought, it was necessary to know the language in which they had been expressed. The countries to which travel was promoted were determined by this basic requirement: thus, Italy was for philosophy and university knowledge, France was for diplomacy and 'courtly graces', and Germany was for the Protestant religion which was beginning to find adherents in England. Italy was a favoured destination for most European travellers influenced by the spirit of the Renaissance. Tudor England was no different, but a point that perhaps may be raised is whether, in this century, England felt a greater need to make a concerted effort to understand Europe and then the world.

In Elizabethan times, given the problems that England faced, at least in the initial years of her reign, access to and knowledge of the intricacies of political manoeuvring on the Continent became much more important. As is well known, Elizabeth had to maintain her realm in the face of tremendous threat from Spain and France, and when there was also a considerable degree of internal opposition. At the same time, it was clear that other countries were gaining from exploration and if England did not participate in such expeditions, she would clearly be left far behind. The spirit of national competition that was becoming more visible in this period led to royal support for the many expeditions in search of the Northwest Passage by explorers such as John Cabot and George Weymouth,[7] to the search for the Northeast Passage (by navigators like the Dutch explorer William Barents), and to Drake for the circumnavigation of the world. The first ultimately resulted in the formation of the Hudson Bay Company, the second in the expansion of the Muscovy and later the Muscovy and Levant Companies, while the third established England's role as a naval power. But it is to be remembered that the goal in the voyages of exploration was always the riches of the East; preferably, at least initially, without stepping on too many political toes, and later, after the defeat of the Spanish Armada, without too much regard being given to possible problems that might come up in the future.[8]

By the end of the 16th century, there was clearly a greater degree of familiarity with both Asia in general and India in particular. Replacing the pseudo-knowledgeable statements of the Septentrion[9] were now details about distances, routes, modes of transport, and, of course, cities. Aleppo and Constantinople had long been familiar names; to these were now added Surat, Cochin, Ormuz, and Gombroon.

Over the course of the period from the 13th to the 17th centuries, the writings show a steady change in both form and content. They start off with a very hazy notion of the east, where India represented the east, but where much of the East was still unknown, untraversed, and different, if not outright dangerous. The familiar had initially been limited to just two things – India itself, and the existence of Christians in the east. Right till the time of Abbé Carré, we have references to 'Christian Arabs' who helped (or did not help) the European travellers. But by his time, the Nestorian community, which had been at the receiving end of considerable criticism by the earlier friars, was hardly even mentioned. Instead, we have information about the Capuchin friars or about the Dominican orders. So, by the 17th century, more recognisable forms of Christianity were clearly well in place.

In the same way, older terms like *India Extra Gangem* or *India Intra Gangem*, or the three Indias, began to be replaced. From the middle of the 16th century in particular, we find a fresh set of names coming up, where Ottoman, "Sophy" (Safavid) and "Mogor" or "Mogol" (Mughal) begin to define Asia to an audience that had already become aware that there was more to Asia than India. In later times, these names became stereotypical labels. China too was known, but as Cathay. Clearly, knowledge of these areas had increased.

In the 17th century, once again, one finds a greater concentration on India. The reasons for this are difficult to determine. One reason many have been the basic familiarity of India, mentally and in reality. Another was possibly the openness of India as compared to China, and the fact that, while sailing, India was the logical landfall, not China. It may also have been the fact that the Indians found it easy to acquire languages and to speak to Europeans in their tongues, current or old – it should be remembered that Vasco da Gama and Albuquerque were addressed in both Hebrew and Latin, languages that were not spoken in India. Alternatively, it could be that Europeans found it easier to acquire Indian languages rather than the Chinese. Whatever the reason, there is no denying that, in the 17th century, India once again acquired a centrality for and in trade and travel.

One aspect of the change can be seen in the kind of writing that become available. Three broad themes can be discerned in the 17th-century writings. The first was that which was concerned with the court, the politics of the court, and with negotiations to get concessions to trade. In the process of the association with the court and the court politics, there was also a certain amount of description of the nobility and of the kinds of 'presents' that had to be given to get the concessions. Part of the description of the court necessarily revolved around visible displays of wealth and ostentation, and, to some extent at least, a highlighting of the distance between the court and the world outside the court. This kind of writing is best exemplified by Thomas Roe, Edward Terry, Francisco Pelsaert, and Francois Bernier. Bernier was, as mentioned earlier, a French physician who was employed in the court of Aurangzeb. He came to India just before the civil war,[10] in the course of which Aurangzeb emerged victorious. But Bernier was probably the least critical of those named here, for he did describe very admiringly the arrangements for justice and the methods of tax collection. On the other hand, he was the first to describe the Mughal nobility as a feudal one and the ambivalence in Europe towards this kind of nobility is reflected in his work.

The second theme is obviously that of trade and merchandise. The writings of John Jourdain, William Methwold, Peter Mundy, Jean-Baptiste Tavernier, John Fryer, Francois Martin, and others clearly reflect the concerns of the English and the French with improving the trade of the companies or the nations with whom they were associated. These accounts should perhaps, strictly speaking, not be called travelogues, but they are a form of travel writing nonetheless. With the exception of Tavernier, all the individuals mentioned travelled as representatives of their respective East India Companies, as they were employees of the companies. All, including Tavernier, were concerned with trade. All the accounts brought together trade, travel, ethnography, and geography. In the process of identifying items of trade, they described the regions where the items were to be found, the people involved in monopolising or trading in them, the various routes that led to and out of the regions of production, and, to some extent, the castes involved in making the items. Another aspect that comes out clearly from their writing is the reality of the state, omnipresent if not omniscient. Monopolies were often at the behest of the state;[11] taxes on the road were collected with permission from the state, and when there were occasional marauding bands on the road, complaints could be and were made to the representative of the state. As European travellers usually did not stay overnight in villages even on their travels, staying rather in smaller towns where there was at least a certain amount of registering of strangers at the entrance, the state was visible here too.

Included in these descriptions was also some discussion on things that were visibly unusual, as for example, the fountain in the garden of the house that the East India Company rented in the city of Surat. Mundy has a detailed description of this fountain, located in the middle of what he called a "Tancke" in the garden. This fountain consisted of a "spowte, which att pleasure is lett to Runn, upon which they add others (as occasion serveth) among the rest, this First six Spowtes running outwards from the Topp of the main spowte."[12] Slightly later, there is a longer description of natural and artificial tanks, and the methods used in India for building the latter. Fryer's account in the same century has descriptions of the bridge that connected the coast near Masulipatnam to the city itself. While he did not categorically mention the technological ability of the Indians to anchor a bridge in swampy ground, the fact that he emphasised the swamp at the coast is indication enough of his sense of perhaps grudging awe. Such descriptions acquired greater focus in the 18th century when the tone of the writings shifted yet again.

The third theme is that of mapping, but not in the Renaissance style of cartography. Rather, these were detailed descriptions of coasts, rivers, currents, and shoals. Building on the earlier Italian and Portuguese *portolani*,[13] these were essentially navigational aids in coastal waters. Thomas Bowrey's

A Geographical Account Of The Countries Round The Bay of Bengal, 1669–1679[14] and at the end of the century, Alexander Hamilton's *A New Account of The East Indies from the years 1688 to 1723*[15] are perhaps the best examples in English of this kind of writing. Bowrey was an independent merchant as well as an occasional pilot[16] for the company ships, and his work can perhaps be seen as indicative of the transition from a travelogue to a navigational aid cum ethnographer's account. He apparently planned to write a detailed Malay-English dictionary, but if he ever did complete the work, it is no longer extant.

Starting with a description of the continent of Asia (which he said, fairly accurately, was 4,320 English miles north to south and 7,500 English miles east to west), he went on to talk about the coast of Coromandel, before giving details about the coasts surrounding the Bay of Bengal. He was careful to specify the points of the coast at which the nomenclature changed: so, from just south of Nagapattinam to the mouth of the Godavari River was the Coromandel coast, and north of the Godavari till the Jagannath temple in Orissa was the Gingelly coast. He did not clearly distinguish the Gingelly and Orissa coasts, but did say that north of Orissa was the Bengal coast. To these descriptions, he added information about the kinds of ships that regularly plied in these waters, merchant communities – he is among the earliest to provide some account of the *Chulias*, a trading community on the Coromandel Coast – the coins current in the kingdom of Golconda, and the continued use of cowrie shells as currency.

Alexander Hamilton's work is another which goes into details about ports, trade, and traders in the ports. The preface to his work states that he was writing in order to correct some of the statements that earlier travellers had made, for, he said, as one who had spent many years in 'those parts' of the world, he was better qualified to describe the east than others who he said were mere 'map-travellers', who had got their reports at 'second or third hands'.[17] Hamilton obviously assumed that there was already a considerable body of knowledge available, and the requirement now was to issue corrections based on personal experience.

With Hamilton, therefore, we get more of an emphasis on eyewitness information. But echoing other contemporaries, such as Fryer, we find in his account, too, a greater degree of criticism. For instance, he stated that his effort to collect information about the places in which he stayed would have been easier if

> Gazetts, and other useful publick Papers were used in those Countries where I travelled, or if I could have read their different histories in their various vernacular Languages, then the general Accounts of their Laws, Religions, Politicks, etc. material Observations, had been much fuller and exacter.[18]

He said that there were undoubtedly laws in the countries he visited, but these were usually customary, and were not necessarily written down. More important, he categorically stated that the rulers were autocratic; thus laws worked fairly well, except when they were "interrupted by the Prince's Order, or stopt by Bribes, to those Governors or Judges who have the Distribution of them"[19] – the first time that we find such a clear statement of autocratic rule and corruption. Many of the statements made in earlier works, like those of Terry, were repeated: a story that Terry recounted, about an African who was captured and taken to England, taught the language, and when taken back, reverted to African customs and dress the minute he set foot on his shore again, is to be found here too, as are statements about the generally barbaric customs followed in Africa. On the other hand, he also stated that the English were the first to try and establish a settlement at the Cape of Good Hope, which they kept for three years, but as those sent were unable to learn the language, the settlement was abandoned: again, information that we do not find anywhere else.

But in many ways, we can also argue that Hamilton's account was a continuation of earlier travelogues, like Varthema or della Valle, who concentrated on the coasts, rather than the hinterlands of the countries they visited. Details are given about the journey around both the Arabian Sea and the Bay of Bengal, with information about the important ports and products found there, as well as about the sailing hazards to be found: for example, Madagascar is once again described as having dangerous rocky and sandy shoals around it.

The English travellers were not the only ones to describe Africa and India in different ways, for in French accounts of the time, too, we find similar descriptions. Jean Chardin, for example, described a reception given by the Shah of Persia in 1673, in which he said that a 'collation' of fruits and food was laid out, and declared that "No other part of the world can afford anything more magnificent and rich or more splendid and bright."[20] The other side – of strange things – is also clear from his account, as when he described a cloud of locusts that he saw when travelling from Shiraz to Gombroon. He reported that some of the locusts fell, and he found that they were the largest he had ever seen. The peasants in the vicinity "gathered them as they fell . . . having gathered, they dry and salt them, after which they live upon them, and sell them to each other very cheap, as they are their common food."[21]

In the 18th century, the tone of the writings changed yet again. For one thing, there were fewer travellers in the 17th-century sense of the word, and more officials. This was the century in which there was more mapping of the countries of Asia, and a clearer marking out of the routes. Information about sailing seasons was no longer necessary; but seasons when storms were likely to occur were noted. Perhaps most interestingly, the products of India began to be examined not from the point of view of profit, but of understanding how they were made, so that they could be replicated in England. This kind of writing can be seen in, for example, the information that was sent back to the Royal Society about Australia's natural flora and fauna, and in India, in the writings of people like Dr. Helenus Scott. Dr. Scott can perhaps be seen as one of the new breed of travellers, who were now 'men of science', who came to India as botanists, zoologists, or, later, anthropologists, in search of 'truth', scientific, rational and western. A classic example of this is the reports sent by Dr. Helenus Scott, who travelled in, particularly, western India in the last decade of the 18th century. He sent regular reports to Sir Joseph Banks, President of the Royal Society, about various aspects of the technology that he saw being used in India. He was, for instance, among the earliest to report on the techniques of glass cutting in the subcontinent. He was particularly interested in the manufacture of dyes in India, and wrote bitterly about the fact that such knowledge in India was "never communicated by writing nor printing nor their experience reduced to general laws by theory."[22] He reported frequently and at great length about the methods used for fixing colours on cloth, and said, early in 1792, that he was "unable to give any theory of the operation of the chief substance that they use and without which they can do nothing."[23] Pointing to the tremendous knowledge that Indians had of the use of vegetable dye, and of changing or enhancing the natural colours by the use of acids and alum, he also said that the exact acid to be used, or the amount of alum required, remained a secret closely guarded by some. This was knowledge that was "never communicated . . . nor their experience reduced to general laws by theory."[24]

A little later, he reported on the use of an astringent for fixing colours, and sent a sample back to the Royal Society for testing by the chemists of that Society. The letter that accompanied this shipment is illustrative of the new mindset. Asking that it be tested, he said that the British chemists would "see at once the general nature of this substance and [the British] artists [would be able to] find how far, by such an agent, they [could] produce the effects to which they have been accustomed."[25] Nor did he limit his reports to the textile industry, for he also sent detailed reports and samples of the steel produced in India, pointing out that it was much harder than that available in Britain at that time. It is to be remembered that he was not alone in furnishing such reports. Francis Buchanan, who travelled through a major part of the Madras Presidency between 1800 and 1802, also gave detailed accounts of the kinds of industries that existed, and the technology that was used. Perhaps in keeping with the general temper of the age, there is still, in these reports, no sign of what has come to be called the colonial mentality – of the innate superiority of the colonial master over the native. On the contrary, there is an acknowledgement of the technical expertise acquired by the Indian craftsmen, and a desire to understand and emulate the same. Scott's reports to Sir Joseph Banks included details about steel manufacturing in India, and he said that the strength of Indian steel lay in the green wood and bellows techniques that were used.[26]

Such travel was aimed at acquiring knowledge, as said earlier, but knowledge was also to be 'useful'. The technology which was described was for those items that were being produced in Britain as well at the same time, and so, what was being done was a comparison of the relative merits and demerits of the produce (and production techniques) of both countries. All the travellers remarked on the intrinsic worth of the Indian products, and encouraged experimentation in Britain to duplicate the results. It is in this that one can see the change to the later colonial system. These accounts can be seen as the beginning of what became a systematic operation later, of colonial takeover of indigenous practices and knowledge. All observers agreed that the difference in the finished product could be understood by rigorous testing by trained chemists. There was, thus, a difference between practical knowledge and theoretical knowledge, and scientific training in the latter would provide the means of understanding and replicating the former. Travel here is seen to have a specific purpose, of acquiring knowledge, and not the light-hearted or profit-based travel of an earlier period.

Accounts of the eastern lands by travellers from the west are clearly wide ranging in both content and form. But what about the reverse – i.e. accounts of the west by travellers from the east? Unfortunately, there are not many of these. In the 13th century, we have a rare reverse journey – Rabban bar Sawma, a Nestorian Christian, travelled westwards from Mongol lands into western Europe, and made his way as far as Bordeaux before returning to his native land.[27] Whether he was following imperial orders, or whether he had already made the decision to travel to Jerusalem, and was given further orders by Kublai Khan, is unclear, but the fact remains that he did travel, and with permission from Kublai. He never got to Jerusalem because the way there was blocked by the movement of various armies, but he did travel further into Europe and met the Pope as well as the King of France. In his narrative, we find very little description of the lands through which he passed. The account in fact gives the impression that, for him, the significance lay in the Pope and Christianity, even though he was a different kind of Christian, and in the fact that despite Nestorianism being considered a heresy, he was well received by the Pope and those whom he met. We do not find anything to compare with, for example, Marco Polo's description of the court of the Khan, or the way in which the Khan handled his administration. There is a very matter-of-fact tone to the entire narrative – he travelled, he visited many places, and he went back, rejoicing that he had finished such a long journey and returned home. The sense of wonder present in contemporaneous European accounts of the east is entirely missing. While we have no indication of the audience for his work, it is possible to speculate that the audience was limited, and that by and large, the people were uninterested in the world outside their confines. Perhaps it is here that we can identify the beginnings of the difference in development of the countries of Europe and Asia. Or else this was a reflection of his reality, that his world was far richer, in every sense of the word, than the one he was visiting.

What was the impact of these accounts? The writings outlined here show a gradual but definite difference in both tone and content, but the nature of readership, at least in the early centuries, is rather difficult to determine. That a readership existed is clear, and is perhaps best proved by the multiple

78 *Recasting the east*

volumes of the Hakluyt Society's publications, which contained *The Principal Navigations, Voyages and Discoveries of the English Nation: Made by Sea or Over Land . . . within the Compasse of these 1500 years*, the first volume of which was published in 1582.[28] Apart from Hakluyt's own work, there was the multi-volume *Hakluytus Posthumus, or Purchas, His Pilgrimes: Containing a History of the World in Sea Voyages and Lande Travells by Englishmen and Others*, published from 1625 onwards. At least one of the ships carrying out the *Third Voyage of the East India Company* (the first English voyage to sail directly to India, in 1607)[29] to India carried a copy of Hakluyt's work; the account of William Keeling, on board a ship called the *Dragon*, states that when they were becalmed off Sierra Leone, and did not have any idea of where exactly to go, he "sent for the Booke". The note in the margin is more important, for it says "M. Hackluites books of Voyages are of great profit. This saved the Company . . . 20000 pounds, which they had bin endamaged if they had returned home, which necessitie had been constrained, if that Booke had not given light."[30] The fictitious *Travels of Sir John Mandeville* definitely had a vast readership and, till probably the 19th century, was regarded as an authentic account. As the author of the narrative had used the accounts of the three friars discussed earlier, these accounts became familiar, although indirectly, to the English-speaking and -reading audience. In the course of the centuries under review, as readership and the desire for accurate knowledge became greater, there was also more translation into different languages – mention has been made earlier of the number of translations of Linschoten's work, and in the 17th century, one of the most frequently translated accounts was that of Francois Bernier. Obviously, all this was against the background of the Renaissance interest in exploration and cartography, and the 'spirit of enquiry' which was the chief characteristic of the age. Travel was not just an expression of one's interest in the world outside, but was also an expression of nationalism, for, as has been pointed out, mapping the world could gradually lead to claiming the world that was being and had been mapped.

A question that perhaps needs to be asked is the extent to which such writings became more widely known and accepted. The *Instructions to Travellers* were clearly geared to an established or an emerging elite, for they assumed that the travels were undertaken for a specific purpose, which was primarily improvement of oneself, but had the added benefit of rendering one fit to serve the nation. Those who went on the travels were usually members of the aristocracy. In some cases, individuals who had come to the notice of the monarchs but were not members of the upper class were promoted.[31] However, the audience for such writing, as a practical set of instructions, would necessarily have been fairly limited. On the other hand, travel itself, or stories of travel, would have attracted a far larger audience. Possibly equally large would have been the audience that knew about travel, but did not want to read travelogues, and preferred the stories of far off lands served up to them through popular fiction or entertainment. It is difficult to determine the extent of dissemination of both travel literature itself and the stories of distant lands through other kinds of popular literature, and, therefore, it is virtually impossible to try and judge the extent to which such writings resulted in a more widespread acceptance of the stereotypes that were being constructed.

That some amount of the ideas of the instructions to travellers, and the contents of some of the travel writing of the late 16th century were known to a non-specialist travel audience is clear from Shakespeare's writings alone. In *The Two Gentlemen of Verona*, Shakespeare has one of his protagonists say "he cannot be a perfect man, Not being tryed, and tutored in the world".[32] Shakespeare in fact provides a great many examples – his *Merchant of Venice*, where he assumed that all his audience would be familiar with the word 'Rialto' and its implications (of stocks and trading); his *Othello*, the Moor, who is nowhere described as a Muslim, and so does imply that there were 'black Christians', or again, *The Two Gentlemen of Verona*, where there is one sentence which seems to find an echo is della Valle later.[33] Some amount of familiarity with the cloth of India seems to come through when he has one of his characters wear a "doublet of changeable taffeta" in the same play. Venice's continued role in seaborne long-distance trade is obviously clear from the *Merchant of Venice*, where Antonio is reported to have ships bound to 'Tripolis', the 'Indies', Mexico, and to England.[34] Perhaps most telling of all is Shakespeare's reference to 'the cursed ship Tyger' in the play Macbeth. The *Tiger* was the name of the ship on which Ralph Fitch sailed and which was believed to have been lost with all hands until Fitch came back to England in the late 1580s. It should be pointed out here that Shakespeare was not unique; similar ideas are to be found in, for example, Ben Jonson's *Volpone* and to a lesser extent in Christopher Marlowe's *The Duchess of Malfi*. Perhaps the most famous of the fictional travelogues was *Gulliver's Travels*, published in 1724, describing the voyages of a traveller between 1699 and 1715.[35] The first two parts of the book do not specify the direction in which Gulliver sailed, but the third voyage first describes him as being attacked by pirates, then marooned on a rocky island off the coast of India and finally reaching Japan. Clear from this section is the continued fascination with tales of the fabulous surrounding India. So, Gulliver is rescued from his island by the flying island of Laputa whose people are renowned for music and mathematics.[36] Again, Fryer comes to mind.

Another set of fabulous stories which perhaps became more popular in the 19th century, and later, were those of Sinbad the Sailor. Two of the threads which run through every one of the Sinbad stories are shipwrecks or being cast away at sea and meeting some kind of fabulous or dangerous animal. Perhaps these were the stories that Shakespeare had in mind when he had Shylock talk about the perils "of waters, winds and rocks". In the 17th century, the export of Shakespeare also began, perhaps not yet to India but definitely on board the ships. The journals of the third voyage to India record that *Hamlet* was performed on 5 September 1607 at Sierra Leone before a mixed audience of Portuguese and local Africans. This was followed by *Richard II* but that was only for the Englishmen on board.[37]

However, there was also a slightly ambivalent attitude to travel. If travel was a window to the world, was that really a world that one wished to inhabit? Travel brought many dangers in its wake – not least that of unfamiliar customs and societies. The east was being better documented, no doubt, but so were the lands to the west of Europe. It must be remembered that there were accounts of travels in the Americas as well, and one of the most widely read accounts was that of the cannibals of the West Indies! Of course, cannibals were in the east as well – accounts did mention cannibalism in Java, as has been said earlier – but these do not seem to have been as widely circulated. To slightly misquote Shakespeare, a serious question was 'what manner of men be these'. This ambivalence is even clearer in Milton's works. Milton was obviously familiar with the writings included in *Purchas, His Pilgrimes*, but in Milton's work, Satan is the traveller, providing temptation, and leading the traveller straight to Hell and damnation. Travel took an individual from the known to the unknown and was dangerous precisely because of that. As the east was governed by ritual and unfamiliar forms of worship, it had to be governed by emotion, not reason, and was therefore doubly dangerous. Such attitudes, when linked to the increasingly censorious statements found in travel writings, as well as to the earlier attitudes to the east, began to manifest themselves in a multitude of ways, many of which ultimately found their way into colonial writings.

Notes

1 We do not know in how many other languages such instructions were published. Guidebooks which provided information about routes and halting places from Germany to different parts of Europe as well as the pilgrim routes were apparently published in German. However, the English instructions appear to have been a little different from the German.
2 Joan-Pau Rubies, *Travel and Technology in the Renaissance: South India through European Eyes, 1250–1625*, Cambridge: Cambridge University Press, 2000, p. 84.
3 Clare Howard, *English Travellers of the Renaissance*, New York, 1913; London: Bodley Head, 1913, p. 3.
4 Sir Henry Ellis, *Original Letters Illustrating English History*, 2 Series, London: Harding, Triphook and Leonard, 1825–1846, pp. i, 110, cited in Ibid., p. 4. The use of the word 'deluded' should be taken note of.
5 Cartaz was the pass issued by the Portuguese to merchants and merchant ships traversing the Indian Ocean world. Any ship could be stopped on the high seas by Portuguese men-of-war and if the cartaz was not displayed, the ship and its cargoes were forfeit to the Portuguese.
6 Mary Augusta Scott (ed., with an introduction and notes), *The Essays of Francis Bacon*, Essay 'On Travaille', New York: Charles Scribner's Sons, 1908, pp. 79–82.
7 John Cabot was commissioned by Henry VII in 1497, while Weymouth sailed on an expedition funded by the East India Company and the Muscovy Company in 1602.
8 At the time of the defeat of the Spanish Armada, they did not think that the Dutch would become their most serious rivals or that the French would subsequently become an even greater problem.

Recasting the east 81

9 A Latin word, used mainly to describe the colder regions of the north of the globe; it is to be found, along with a whole lot of other geographical terms, in Mandeville, as well as in other more authentic texts. Also used by Shakespeare in *Henry VI*.
10 This was the war among the four sons of Shah Jahan, Dara Shukoh, Murad Baksh, Aurangzeb, and Shah Shuja, for control of the empire. Aurangzeb emerged victorious and on getting the throne of Delhi imprisoned his father in Agra fort until the latter's death seven years later.
11 For example, a nobleman Mir Muhammad Taqi was given the monopoly for money changing in Masulipatnam in 1621, something that the English complained about at length to no effect. See William Foster (ed.), *The English Factories in India*, Oxford: Clarendon Press, 1906–1927 in particular, Vol. 1 and 2.
12 Ibid., p. 26.
13 *Portolani* were charts that were used as aids to navigation initially by the Italians in the 13th century, and later by the Spanish and the Portuguese. Usually oriented to a fixed point, they were used extensively initially in the Mediterranean and the Black Sea, and later, by the Spanish and the Portuguese, in the Atlantic and Indian Oceans as well.
14 Hakluyt Society, 1903, Indian edition, Munshiram Manoharlal, 1997.
15 Alexander Hamilton, *A New Account of the East Indies: Being the Observations and Remarks o Capt. Alexander Hamilton, from the Year 1688, to 1723*, the second edition, London, 1739; reprint, New Delhi: Asian Educational Services, 1995.
16 The word 'pilot' or variations of the Asian word *nakhuda* meant those who were responsible for actually guiding a ship into a river or into the harbour. They were familiar with the intricacies of river or coastal navigation and were therefore responsible for making sure that the boats did not get grounded or wrecked on any of the shoals.
17 Hamilton, op. cit., p. xiv.
18 Ibid., p. xvii.
19 Ibid., p. xviii.
20 James Richards (ed.), *Sir John Chardin's Travels in Persia*, 2000, google.com, accessed 24 October 2014.
21 *The World Displayed: of, a Collection of Voyages and Travels Selected from the Writers of All Nations*, 8 Vols., Vol. 7, Philadelphia: Travels of Sir John Chardin, 1796. Accessed through the Internet Archive, 24 October 2014.
22 Dharampal, ed., *Indian Sciences and Technology in the Eighteenth Century: Some Contemporary European Accounts*, New Delhi: Impex, 1971, p. 252–259.
23 Ibid.
24 Ibid.
25 Ibid.
26 These methods seem to have died out shortly after, and our information on the bellows comes now primarily from his description.
27 E.A. Wallis Budge (tr. and ed.), *The Monks of Kublai Khan, Emperor of China, or: The History of the Life and Travels of Rabban Sawma, Envoy and Plenipotentiary of the Mongol Khans to the Kings of Europe*, London: The Religious Tract Society, 1928, www.google .com, Accessed 15 October 2014.
28 Subsequent editions of the volumes did not say until 1600 CE and merely said Voyages, Travels and Discoveries of the English Nation.
29 The first voyage, under Sir James Lancaster, reached the Malacca Straits and Bantam, and set up two factories at Bantam and in the Moluccas. The Second Voyage, under Sir Henry Middleton, also went to Bantam.
30 Samuel Purchas, *Hakluytus Posthumus, or Purchas His Pilgrimes in Twenty Volumes*, Vol. 2, University of Glasgow, 1905, p. 503. Accessed through the Internet Archive, 7 October 2014.

82 Recasting the east

31 For example, John Mason, the son of a cowherd, who was studying at Oxford and came to the notice of Henry VIII at Oxford and was sent by Henry VIII to Paris for further studies. But we do not know if he was also given a copy of the instructions. Ibid., p. 13.
32 Act I, Sc. iii.
33 Act V, Sc. iv, where one of the characters says "How use doth breed a habit in a man!" Della Valle's statements have been cited earlier.
34 Merchant of Venice, Act I, Sc. iii.
35 In the 1726 reprint of the book a picture of the hero was provided with engraved below it the words "*splendide mendex*", which can be translated as wonderful or glittering liar. See Daniel Carey, "Truth, Lies and Travel Writing", Carl Thompson (ed.), *The Routledge Companion to Travel Writing*, London: Routledge, 2016, p. 3.
36 It is tempting to argue that Jonathan Swift was familiar with Fryer's description of the ability of Indians to "arithmetize to the meanest fraction", but rather difficult to prove! In the same way it would be nice if one could prove that John Bunyan's 'Vale Perilous' in *The Pilgrim's Progress* was derived from Mandeville's vale perilous.
37 Richmond Barbour, *The Third Voyage Journals: Writings and Performance in the London East India Company, 1607–10*, Basingstoke: Palgrave Macmillan, 2009, pp. 15–16.

6 Anchoring the 'Orient'

Travellers covered long distances, but travel accounts can be said to have had as long a journey. These accounts take the reader from myths to reality, from fabulous stories to accurate information, from information on products and peoples to customs and religion, and from a certain degree of wonder at the reality of those worlds, to a sense of (sometimes rather smug) superiority at the differences that existed. Travel and travel narratives mapped this journey from the exotic to the pedestrian, from the wonderful to the disgusting, to be subsumed into colonial formations and colonial writings, and then to add substance to those perceptions.

What was the impact of these accounts? A difference in both tone and content can be clearly seen in the course of the period under review. There is clearly a continued engagement with the many travel narratives. Mention has already been made of the multiple volumes of the Hakluyt Society's publications. The long enduring popularity of Mandeville's *Travels* is yet another indication of this. But what is perhaps even more significant is the number of times travel accounts were re-published or translated and published within a few years of the publication of the original account. Bernier's *Travels in the Mogul Empire*, Marco Polo's account, and Linschoten's narrative were all translated from the original into English as well as other European languages, and these translations were published within twenty years of the original book. At one level, one can see this as 'book history'; but it also speaks volumes about the interest that such narratives generated in a large audience.

As has been discussed earlier, the 'east' began to be formulated in Europe from the early medieval age itself. Medieval Europe was largely cut off from the rest of the known world for quite some time between the decline of the Roman Empire and the Crusades. Contacts did exist throughout this period, but were restricted to the select few, often located mainly in Italy. Within Europe itself, with the establishment of Byzantium, a difference began to develop between the Latinate and the Greek cultures. The latter, as exemplified by Byzantium, was first seen as different, and later as hostile, primarily because of the nature of Christianity followed, for Byzantium practised the form of Christianity that came to be known as the 'Orthodox Church', rather than the Latinate version.

The ambivalence towards Byzantium began to manifest itself from the middle of the 10th century. The change is perhaps most clearly identifiable in the series of negotiations that took place to try and arrange a marriage between the son of Otto I, Holy Roman Emperor, and a Byzantine princess, Anna. The Bishop of Cremona, Liutprand, was sent as Otto's ambassador to conduct the negotiations, and it is from his writings that one can identify the gap that was beginning to appear between 'east' and 'west'.

Liutprand first visited Constantinople in 949 CE at which time he seems to have had no serious problems to face. He came back from this first visit with a supply of the purple cloth for which Byzantium was famous. The second visit in 968 CE was, however, considerably more problematic. Nicephorus, Emperor of Byzantium, had now begun to question Otto's claim to the title of Holy Roman Emperor, for, as the ruler of Byzantium and the inheritor of the legacy of the Roman Empire (to some extent), he claimed that he could be the only Roman Emperor. Unfortunately, it was at this time that Nicephorus began to be addressed by the Pope as the 'emperor of the Greeks' rather than as Emperor of Byzantine. Probably not surprisingly, Nicephorus found this highly insulting. Negotiations for the marriage fell through, and, worse still, at the end of this visit, Liutprand was not allowed to take back any purple cloth. He was told that it was only 'fitting' that a "distinction of dress should belong to those alone who surpass other nations in wealth and wisdom".[1] Liutprand's report to Otto, on his return, makes for very interesting reading, for he said,

> So, you see, they judge all Italians, Saxons, Franks, Bavarians, Swabians – in fact all other nations – unworthy to go about clothed in this way. Is it not indecent and insulting that these soft, effeminate, long-sleeved, bejewelled and begowned liars, eunuchs and idlers should go about in purple, while our heroes, strong men trained to war, full of faith and charity, servants of God, filled with all virtues, may not![2]

Nor was this his only peroration. He was extremely contemptuous of the look of the king as well. Quoting a Sicilian bishop, Hippolytus, he declared that

> The king of the Greeks wears long hair, a tunic, long sleeves, a hood; is lying, crafty, without pity, sly as a fox, proud, falsely humble, miserly, and greedy; lives on garlic, onions, and leeks, and drinks bath-water. The king of the Franks, on the contrary, is beautifully shorn; wears a garment not at all like a woman's garment, and a hat; is truthful, without guile, merciful enough when it is right, severe when it is necessary, always truly humble, never miserly; does not live on garlic, onions and leeks so as to spare animals, and, by not eating them, but selling them, to heap money together.[3]

One needs to look no further to identify the hardening of attitudes. It is interesting that many of the pejorative terms used by the Bishop – soft, effeminate, idlers – recur fairly regularly in late 18th-century and 19th-century writings. 'Eunuchs' and 'idlers' were terms most often used in connection with the Ottoman empire in later times, while 'soft' and 'effeminate' were often used in connection with Indians.

In the 10th century itself, the spread of Islam, and later the Crusades, added to the process of identifying the east within broadly religious terms. Islam had entered the Mediterranean world with the Arabs, when they conquered Cyprus in the 8th century. They consolidated their control of the former Roman lake with the conquest of Palermo in 831 CE. In the course of the 10th century, with Palermo as base, they gradually captured all of Byzantium's ports in southern Italy and Greece, and in the process managed to take over the trade of the Mediterranean.[4] This, then, was one of the earliest formulations of 'the East': people who could not be understood, much less trusted.

But it should be remembered that representations of the east were multiple. However, whatever the description, the one thing that remained constant was the wealth of the eastern lands. Mathew Paris, the Benedictine monk and historian, stated that

> There are only seven climes in the whole extent of the world, namely those of the Indians, Ethiopians or Moors, Egyptians, Jerusalemites, Greeks, Romans, and French, and there are none so remotely situated in the whole of the habitable part of the world, that merchants will not find their way amongst them.[5]

The friars made their way into these 'climes', unfamiliar to them, undoubtedly, but not to the mercantile classes of Europe. Jewish traders like Benjamin of Tudela had visited Europe, Asia, and Africa in the 12th century, before Marco Polo or the friars. He has left a fairly detailed account of his travels. He travelled from Tudela in northern Spain, probably by land to France, then by sea to Genoa. Then he went overland to the south of Italy, crossed to Greece, and made his way to Constantinople. From Constantinople, he went by sea to the eastern Mediterranean, by land to Jerusalem and finally got to Basra. Thereafter, he sailed through the Persian Gulf, around Arabia, and up the Red Sea to make his way back to the Mediterranean and returned to Spain. Though he did not travel to India and China, he did know about the lands further to the east of Persia. Benjamin was probably among the first to describe the subjects of Prester John at a time when the name of Prester John was just becoming known in Europe. Interestingly, he described the Mongols as the subjects of Prester John, something that seems to be have been unknown to the Friars who went into Mongol lands later, for they make no mention of Prester John in this connection.[6] While his frame of reference was the existence of Jewish settlements in all these places, his account seems more to be a matter of verifying that they still existed and lived in these regions, rather than any 'discovery' of the people, either of the areas that he went to, or those further away that he knew of.

Between the search for the lands of Prester John, the increasing interest in exploration from the 15th century and the Spanish and Portuguese voyages of discovery, knowledge about the world began to flow back into Europe. The number of writings on the non-European world increased as did greater knowledge about the products of this world. Donald Lach's immense work on *Asia in the Making of Europe* is well known. He has pointed out that the

> reactions in scholarly Europe to the opening of the East were conditioned by the character of the disciplines involved as well as by the reigning intellectual conflicts. . . . As a group the practitioners [of the different disciplines] were more receptive than the theoreticians to the new products and information of Asia and found little trouble in accommodating them.[7]

If the search for the lands of Prester John was one part of the voyages of discovery, this search was only partly driven by the desire to find this great Christian King. Far more important was the belief that he ruled over rich lands. The desire for profit was probably much greater than the call of religion. As has been said earlier, the wealth of India, representing the east, had never been forgotten. Travel into the Mongol lands perhaps showed that these lands did not provide too many opportunities for trade and profit, but to the east lay China and to the south, India. Acquisition of knowledge about both these lands added to the existing belief about the 'fabulous' wealth available here.

The idea of wealth is perhaps most clearly seen in the writings of Odoric and Marco Polo in the earlier period, and then in the accounts of the 17th century. It is to be remembered that most of those who came to the east, particularly after the middle of the 16th century, were merchants, and were naturally primarily concerned with the produce of the countries they visited. In the process of establishing bases for trade, they discovered the networks of trade, family, religion or just continuous contact that already existed. Neither the traveller nor the European merchants had access to these networks, but, as outsiders, they could describe and often resent the fact that they were excluded. The difference between 'them' and 'us' began to be both noticeable and noticed. The noticing of difference was obviously a two-way process, which is perhaps most clear from Conti's remark about Europeans having only one eye, which has been discussed earlier.[8] The Europeans, however, did believe that they were seeing with both eyes and both were objective. They were outsiders, and at least initially, the view from outside was not a judgemental one. However, the difference was underlined, and this difference was increasingly also defined as exotic.

'Exotic' was a convenient umbrella word, including everything from climate to religion, from skin colour to jewellery, from wild animals to oriental despots. The word added to the perception of the 'other', for it also evoked memories of past writings and descriptions of the Orient – the lands of wealth, the lands of 'different' people (physically shorter, and with multiple skin tones, from yellow through brown to black), and with specific reference to India, a great deal more. India was perhaps better known to the west than China or Japan, and more importantly, the 'land of the Indies' remained part of the common consciousness of Europe all through the medieval period. India had never been forgotten in Europe, and India had been variously represented in different times – as the end of the known world (Alexander), the cause of the drain of Rome's wealth (Pliny), the place of the martyrdom of St. Thomas (medieval Church historiography), the land of "Prester John" (in the same and in the post-Renaissance period as well), and, of course, the land of unimaginable wealth (17th-century travel accounts) and finally (in the 19th century) as the poor, uncivilised nation, lacking rationality, Christianity, and all those 'civilising' features that made England great. I would like to point out here that the idea of Indians as irrational is not something that makes its appearance only in the 19th century: Edward Terry's major complaint about the "Mahometans and Gentiles" has already been cited.

Travel by this time was clearly an activity that allowed one to 'look upon' and 'look into' without being 'part of'. In other words, travel and the traveller allowed one to examine from the outside and therefore retain a sense of objectivity, something that was being more talked about in 16th- and 17th-century Europe. The objective onlooker was necessarily one who maintained a conscious distance between himself and the world he was describing. Again, Terry becomes the example as when he juxtaposes "pleasant Fountaynes" with "venimous and pernicious Creatures".[9] The gardens were a luxury, consciously created in the middle of a rather hostile landscape. Something that begins to come out here is the idea of the Oriental monarch as one very distant from his subjects, and therefore as despotic, autocratic, one on whom there is no check, and one who creates an artificial landscape to which his subjects do not have access. So he lived in artificial surroundings, tailored to his comforts while his subjects stayed in penury. Implied also is the contrast with England, where Parliament was already a well-established institution, which could control the monarch when necessary. Roe's account also picks up this idea, as well as that of the alien, as, for example, when he compares the Mughal Darbar with a theatre, as has been mentioned earlier. Englishmen, he seems to be implying, had a greater sense of dignity and pride than the Indians, who made spectacles of themselves. Added to this are the descriptions of the magnificence of the courts, as well as the kinds of things given as presents. It was pointed out that Indians did not need the goods brought by the Europeans; instead, lists were given of "looking glasses, toys and other such small items" that were given to the king and the nobles. The King's desire for such things had nothing to do with his wealth, of which he had an immense amount, but was rather indicative of the irresponsibility and childishness of the king, who was more concerned with amusement than weighty matters of state. The notion of wealth too plays a role in such representations, for the impression conveyed was that wealth created the façade of magnificence, based on the exploitation of the subjects. This exploitation was possible because the King owned all the land, and so the idea of despotic monarchy was reiterated. In both Roe and later, Bernier, there is clearly visible the horror of the possibility of the king owning all the land. The background of 17th-century Europe foregrounded the importance of an independent, landed aristocracy, something that they could not identify in India. Such images constructed an idea of an empire based on distance between the monarch and his subjects, and on the maintaining of that distance to keep control. The people had to submit to the tyranny of the monarch, for they did not even have their lords to help them. Nor were they even aware of the lack, for they had been conditioned to accept subordination.

What comes through in these accounts is that the material reality is the only one that can be clearly grasped, defined, and later quantified. Many of those who came to India from the 16th century onwards were concerned with India's trade and so most accounts are also in some sense merchants' handbooks. Detailed lists of commodities to be found at the places visited by these travellers as well as methods of purchase are usually included in the accounts, as, for example, in Ralph Fitch's description of Patna and Ahmedabad, or Duarte Barbosa's account of the way in which the Zamorin of Calicut welcomed foreign traders. However, underlying the lists of commodities and places is a sense of their being located somewhere both exotic and alien.[10] Here, then, is one of the first forms of marginalisation. Europe is real, for it has meaning, and therefore imparts meaning to its people. Identity is clear – it is rooted in the nation-state and the language (this is particularly true of the English and the French). Indian commodities are real enough, for they are required in Europe, and both that need, and the fact that they are tangible, imparts sufficient meaning to them; but the country that generates these commodities is not, and therefore, to use the word again, is 'exotic' – or perhaps 'fabulous'.

The travellers' accounts reflect one of the concerns of the European Renaissance, that of cartography. All accounts have descriptions of routes from one place to another, whether by land or by sea. Perhaps the best examples are Tavernier's description of the route from Surat to Masulipatnam via Burhanpur, and Bowrey's book itself, called *A Geographical Account of the Countries around the Bay of Bengal, 1659–1669*. The description served the dual purpose of information for merchants, and perhaps it is one manifestation of the idea that describing or providing knowledge allowed one to claim that environment. Recent researches have shown the hegemonic nature of such explorations, for mapping the world implied control over the world that was mapped. While I am not arguing that such descriptions were, at this time, clearly geared towards power in political terms, they did provide to subsequent travellers a sense of the familiar in an unfamiliar world. The east, in other words, was dangerous, and later required the mediation of the west to bring it under control. This theme was picked up by the later colonial writings to emphasise difference. The difference was of two kinds – (i) control as that to be imposed and (ii) different kinds of control on different people. It could then be argued that it was colonialism that brought about order and 'regulation' – it is perhaps significant that many of the instructions were termed 'Regulations'.

As said earlier, the writings show a steady change in both tone and content. In the 13th century, there was clearly a curiosity and a desire to know more. Thus, Johannes de Plano Carpini described the customs of the Tartars, such as the belief that fire was not to be touched with a knife, for fear that that would "take away the head or force from the fire", and that fire itself was sacred.[11] He also praised the unity of the Mongols, and said that Christians had to unite to face the threat, and to be well armed,[12] preferably using the Mongol methods of sharpening and hardening arrowheads. Visible here is an appreciation both of Mongol technology and tactics in warfare, as well as a clear-sighted understanding of the shortcomings of the Europeans in the face of this threat. Rubruquis focussed on slightly different aspects, and so described their methods of travel and food. In his account, there is an attempt to explain the unfamiliar in terms familiar to his reader, as, for instance, when he compared the share of milk given to the Duke to the feudal practices prevalent in Syria. Odoric had the advantage of travelling in lands that the Europeans knew about, and, so, could mention things like the area defended by Porus against Alexander without having to explain.

However, travel writing began to identify certain characteristics which later seem to have been used as stereotypes. Carpini was the first to describe the physical appearance of the Mongols, something that was not picked up by Odoric or by Marco Polo. Linschoten specified the skin colour of the people of Africa and India without linking colour to character, something which first Herbert and later Fryer did in the 17th century. At the same time, it must be reiterated that India had for many centuries been more familiar territory. India's products were sufficiently well known in Europe, and stories about India were current enough, that, after the 15th century in particular, what was sought was more knowledge of the variety of products and the ways in which these products could be accessed by the Europeans, rather than just the reiteration of the 'marvels' of India.

Therefore, we see in the accounts yet another shift. Linschoten, when going along the west coast, talked of the people of 'Ballegaut' – the western ghats – and about their bringing goods down to the coast. He was clear that these were not goods produced on the coast but brought there, even if he did not know where they were manufactured or grown. Barbosa, talking of the Malabar region, stated that the king assigned a broker to the foreign merchants and these brokers had access to the interior production areas. Tavernier in the next century described the processes of production and the areas of production.

In the process of learning how and from where to source the material required in Europe, the need to understand political structures began to be felt. So, while 15th-century accounts do not mention political history, from the 16th century onwards narratives invariably began with the history of the ruling dynasties. Even then, the early accounts such as those of Fitch focussed more on the size of the armies and the use of elephants in the army – there seems to have been a continuing fascination with the use of elephants in war, perhaps dating back to the stories of Hannibal crossing the Alps with elephants. Linked to this political history was something else that began to be seen as unique. This was that, in the 13th century, when the rest of the known world had fallen prey to the Mongols, India had not – so, was there something about or in India that held firm, or was it just the size and numbers that prevented the Mongols from conquering India? India thus moved from being 'familiar' and therefore 'safe', to 'unique' and safe – unique because she had not succumbed, and safe for the same reason. To this idea of 'unique' was added India's wealth. This 'wealth' encompassed every aspect written about in earlier times – skin colour and physical features of the people, the cities and their teeming multitudes, the enormous range of cloth, the visible luxury, and, of course, the wealth that she possessed. In every possible way, India seemed both different and better off than the countries from which these travellers came.

It was the 'different', ultimately, that captured the imagination. Difference was finally narrowed down to three things – the women, the wealth (especially as seen in the courts), and the religion. It is with the women that we also start getting our clearest hints of the future turn that accounts of the Orient would take. Increasingly, the accounts of the 17th century imply some kind of bondage when they describe the jewellery that the women wore – anklets like fetters, necklaces like ropes, for example. The later rather prurient fascination with the harem also begins to be visible now, where, in the account of Nicholas Whittington, it is mentioned that one member of his party, by name Steele, was allowed into the harem by a eunuch. On entry, his head was covered by a thick cloth, so that "he should not see the Women (which he might heare as hee passed, and once also saw them, the Eunuch purposely putting on a thinner cloth over his head)."[13] Visible in this passage are the elements that became part of any description of the harem in later times – the permission given to one man to enter, on some pretext or the other, and the 'sly' eunuch conniving at the attempts of that man to get a glimpse of the 'forbidden' women. The reverse is also true, as for example, when Roe said that the women made holes in the windows behind which they stood, so that they could see him clearly. The fascination with the harem continued, as can be seen from Manucci's account of the gossip about the princess Jahanara's lovers and the way in which one escaped from the harem. Women as the 'power behind the throne' also make an occasional appearance, as for instance, in François Catrou's[14] statement that women were the 'cabinet council of the Mogol'.

The kings were visibly wealthy, and this is something that comes through even in the accounts of the Mongols. Both Carpini and Rubruquis mention that the Mongols had gold, silver, and silk cloth, and there is an underlying tone of wonder, that a people who did not have a city life, and were essentially nomads, should yet have access to such tangible proofs of wealth. The wealth of India has been described in sufficient detail previously, so there is no need here to reiterate it. However, in India, with the wealth, there is the added feature of the king's display of wealth. Also identifiable in the descriptions of the court and court politics, is the later development of the idea of the 'Oriental Despot', concerned with himself and his position, but totally divorced from the 'real' world outside his palace.

If on the one hand there was a conspicuous display of wealth, another dimension of the 'difference' of the eastern kings was provided by descriptions of the King's cruelty. The kings were reported to enjoy spectacles involving fights between elephants, and men and elephants (mounted or otherwise); and Jahangir in particular was said to 'delight' in seeing "men executed, and torne with Elephants."[15] Condemned people were given the choice of animal to fight with, reminiscent of the circuses of ancient Rome. No comparison is made with similar bloodthirsty sports that were popular in England at the time, but here, these sports are in some way linked to the innate barbarism of the Easterner. The Emperors were also reported to keep such animals in cages, for there is often mention of lions, tigers, and wolves, as well as alligators in ponds – all in the palaces.

Yet another aspect of difference was shown through descriptions of the King's greed. Escheat was seen as one manifestation of this, as was Akbar's taking all the wealth that his mother had possessed after her death. The giving of presents at court was further proof of this. On the other hand, such accounts of gift-giving were also presented alongside descriptions of the King's generosity, in charitable and other activities. What one gets, therefore, is a slowly built picture of Kings who were subject to sudden whims and fancies, who had the means to indulge them, and against whom no voice could be raised. Occasionally, there is also mention of justice on 'rational' grounds, but by and large, dispensation of justice was seen to be arbitrary. All these elements feature over and over again in later constructions of the 'Orient'. It is, in fact, noticeable that, in all the descriptions of the kingdom of Akbar and Jahangir, the one by Ralph Fitch is perhaps the one that shows the least signs of the concept of the 'other' that begins to make its presence felt.

Religion was the final aspect of the unfamiliar. To travellers brought up in the Christian tradition, idol worship began as something strange, as can be seen in, for example, the accounts of Friar Odoric, Pietro della Valle, and Peter Mundy, but not as something deserving castigation. With both Odoric and Mundy there is an attempt to give descriptions of the idols in slightly more familiar terms, so Odoric compared the statue he saw in Ma'abar to the idols of St. Christopher and Mundy talked about an idol being made with a decoration on the head rather like a hat. Over the course of the period under review, acceptance of idol worship began to be seen as contemptible. When religion was linked to rituals like sati, the strangeness of the land was clear, as were the customs, and this strangeness was further illustrated by descriptions of wild animals. It is interesting that many of these accounts seem to imply that the dangers were ever-present, and apparently just waiting for an unwary move on the part of the stranger to entrap him! These 'dangers' needed first to be described, so that they could be identified; then harnessed, so that they would cease to be dangerous; and finally, degraded, so that they would be exposed as being intrinsically worthless. It can be argued that this was the process by which colonialism acquired its mastery over both the mental and the physical worlds of the 'east' – constructed through writing, and then taken over as subordinate.

The 18th-century 'discovery of Hinduism' by the British tended to reinforce such images, with the difference that representations of Indian women and India began to overlap. For example, when William Jones talked of Śakuntala as a 'child of nature',[16] implicit in this was the notion of a people at a primary level of civilisation, and therefore unconcerned with the norms of morality that governed the 'civilised' world. Such a description had the additional advantage of picking up the earlier idea of the childishness of the kings. Indians had none of the features that distinguished Europeans. They did not have the language, of course, nor did they have the physical characteristics. They were shorter, more delicate, and therefore less 'manly', and most importantly, lacking in rationalism. This lack manifested itself, first, in the lack of separation between church and state, and second, in the religion itself. Hinduism was increasingly divided into two, the 'practical and popular belief' and the 'speculative and philosophical doctrines'. The latter found its best expression in mysticism – which, divorced from everyday material life, was esoteric. Till as late as the early years of the 20th century, Hinduism could be defined as the "religion of feminine natures. Enthusiastic surrender, a delicate capacity for feeling, soft passiveness, are its characteristics. Prophetic religion, on the contrary, has an unmistakably masculine character, ethical severity, bold resoluteness, and disregard of consequence, energetic activity".[17]

What I am trying to argue here is that travel accounts began to create a 'landscape of imagination' which had itself been created by memories of earlier stories and some historical reality. Herodotus' gold-digging ants, the wealth of Persia as known to the Greeks, the knowledge of strange products that came from India (including cotton and pepper), and Alexander's conquests – all added to this landscape. Imaginary worlds are often better when they can be located in an identifiable region, the more distant from one's familiar surroundings, the greater the scope for fantasy. The east became peopled and clothed in all kinds of stories. From Mandeville's cockodrills and gerfaunts, to Sinbad's Great Roc or his flying islands; from trees which had wool to diamonds that were created by the dew of heaven – all these added to the fabulous east. When travel began, there were multiple objectives – adventure, knowledge and profit. Perhaps the acquiring of knowledge about the lack of the fantastic creatures was a let-down; but the travel itself provided adventure enough. The landscapes of imagination or of memory were no longer necessary, for the reality was often strange enough and fantastic enough, and had the added merit of being true. In the process, what happened was perhaps similar to what Paul Carter[18] has said about mapping. He has suggested that surveyors, in their travels, placed landscapes "within a discourse of fact and location that can rob the land of its own meaning." So, he argues, there is a transformation in the way in which land is first experienced by the surveyor, and the way it is understood through his representation, by 'a reader who is not present.'[19]

The reader was thus exposed to a range of knowledge, and possibly a bewildering amount of information, not the least of which was trying to locate this nebulous 'east'. The 'east' moved from just beyond the Danube and Russia in the 13th century to India and China in the 16th century. In those centuries, the boundaries of the familiar and the unfamiliar world gradually shifted, but it is noticeable that India consistently remained much more familiar and accessible. The words 'mysterious' or 'secretive' were very rarely applied to the country, and more often to the people – the Brahmans, particularly – in contrast to China, where both land and people were unfathomable (this is an attitude that persists). History and historiography seem to have provided a sense of location and continuity. Thus, Odoric talked of the old name of Tauris, and of the legends of Alexander, and Linschoten located his account within the tradition of the Greek writings on India. But as historiography of China was rather more limited, this could be applied only to India. The 'east' could then be subdivided into 'middle' and 'far' in addition to India. The forms of subordination implicit in colonialism could draw on all these aspects, and recast them in an altogether different form. These centuries thus map the shift, first in location, then in thought, and finally in terms of inferior and superior.

A 'tale', as Shakespeare famously said, is full of 'sound and fury', 'signifying nothing'. The last is obviously not true of these travellers, though one can say that the sound and fury exist, perhaps in something as simple as in the descriptions of the music played in the religious processions. They are nevertheless 'tales' that seem to follow the traditional 'once upon a time . . . and they lived happily ever after' pattern – even if the 'happily ever after' does not include all the cast of characters described. There are elements of the fantastic in all the accounts, but like any good tale, they are founded on a bedrock of a tangible, identifiable reality. In a fairy tale, that which is real may be the king, queen, and the wealth that they control. In these accounts, there is definitely a king, a kingdom, and immense wealth. All are described in very precise terms – the king's genealogy, the size of his kingdom, and the range of its products. The element of the exotic, which in the fairy tale may be provided by witches, demons, and/or a variety of adventures, is here provided by inserting descriptions of the exotic into the mundane. Thus, with trade, we have lions and tigers; with descriptions of war, the use of elephants as instruments of war; and with descriptions of the people, the dress and jewellery worn by women. It was through these devices that an 'Orient' was constructed – one immensely rich, but alien, and often beyond understanding. As the element of the strangeness was heightened, difference visible in the countries came to be transferred to the people and practices, to create an 'Other', which needed no further explanation or description.

Many indications of the expanding horizons of knowledge can be seen. In modern times, Merriam Webster's online dictionary lists the inclusion of a number of words into the English language in the middle of the 16th century. Even a cursory reading gives us words like crocodile, Indian elephant, Tsar, Czar, Polish, European, and Bohemian to name just a few. These words were both names and labels, for they pointed not only to a world outside England, but also to a larger one beyond what had been known until then. If there was an Indian elephant, then there was probably another elephant as well with different characteristics and different features; and Polish and Bohemian were perhaps not the same as European. The act of naming, and later the conscious act of mapping, defining, and classifying, began to indicate both the superior knowledge of and a superior ability to do any or all of these things. Processes of subordination perhaps began with naming and ended with compartmentalisation.

As a genre, travel writing acquired greater importance from the 16th century. The world could be brought to one's own doorstep through such writing, and with no more effort required than going out to purchase a book, one could get accurate information about the world. It was thus a window to the world, which could be enjoyed either first or second hand. Mention has already been made of the ambivalence to travel, with the straight and narrow path sometimes being recommended over the adventurous one. As travelogues shifted from being fables to accounts, travel narratives had to provide proof of veracity so that they could be taken seriously. The traveller may have been motivated by curiosity or a desire for adventure, but without proving that he 'knew' because he had 'seen' and verified, he could not stake a claim to fame. Reputation could be built and profit acquired (perhaps in material terms as well) through such narratives. As the tale moved from a story to description, it became an account which could lead others along the same paths, perhaps to more material profit, but they would never detract from the first traveller's claim to have beaten the track.

Fabulous stories of course had a readier audience and so the travellers could not give up altogether any mention of the fantastic. But as said earlier, exotic became much more used as a term of description than fabulous, which was finally mythical. In Shakespeare's *Othello*, for example, we find both points of view; Desdemona was fascinated by Othello's tales of 'antres vast', cannibals, and men with heads between their shoulders. Iago called these 'fantastical lies'.[20] Stories of men with dog heads and men with their heads in their chests had been around for a long time, and had also sometimes been seen in maps,[21] but mapping too now began to be more accurate.

From the 16th century onwards, travel also began to be more purposeful. Very few travelled, or could afford to travel, for the sake of travel alone. The traveller was almost certainly infused with a desire for self-aggrandisement, even if it was only to return home and prove to everyone that he had gone 'where no man had gone before.' The worlds to be explored lay both to the west and east of Europe, but it should be remembered that these worlds were not yet fixed geographically. It could be said that in geographical terms, the west was easier to define, for it lay across the ocean. The east was more difficult, as it was known and unknown, explored and unexplored, and far from being clearly identified. Russia could therefore remain as 'east' as China farther away, while India remained India and Africa remained Africa. These narratives helped in the process of anchoring the east through a variety of mechanisms including physical description, descriptions of material wealth, customs, cultures, languages, and religions. All were unfamiliar, but all became familiar and perhaps commonplace in the course of these centuries. The purpose/s of the different travelogues were of course different, for the kind of writing that emerged out of the concerns of the Crusades, for example, were clearly different from those that drove the writings of the merchants and adventurers of a later time. These last, in turn, were also distinct from the 'official' writings of the 17th and 18th centuries. However, the point of this work is to try and locate these many different purposes in a different framework, one not contemporary to the writings, but used, partially, and with a different focus, in another time and with a different purpose.

One part of this shift, from curiosity to knowledge, was of course mapping. Simon Ryan has pointed out that maps "aggressively construct the observer as a viewer in space, to whom the earth is fully revealed."[22] Exploration, he argues, defined the landscape as much as the explorer; and it is this aspect of travel literature that I am trying to highlight. The iconic *Star Trek* has the sentence "to boldly go where no man has gone before' – in many ways, this defined travel. To go to strange, new lands, to know them, and then to transmit that knowledge: that made the traveller's voice authoritative. The authority remained even after the traveller himself had died, so the definition could be used for any purpose, in all times and spaces.

Travelogues remain popular till today, but the kinds of travelogues of the period under review were different in many ways, not the least of which was the aspect of the unfamiliar. The acquiring of knowledge which could translate into profit, as reputation, as well as in more concrete material terms, would also have played a part in the writing of the narrative. Therefore, the onus of proof of having spoken the truth was on the traveller. Proof could be supplied by expanding, negating, or dismissing altogether accounts of those who had gone before. But in the process, what we can see is some continuity of description, such as in the accounts of storms at sea, of different kinds of fish (both predatory and edible), or in the descriptions of people, which in the course of time became so accepted that they were no longer worthy of

96 Anchoring the 'Orient'

mention. These were 'truth', but they were also stereotypes which contributed to different notions of the Orient.

Today's world is 'known' to many, so today the travelogues themselves have become a 'curiosity'. The worlds that they describe have ceased to exist, but the writings give us a sense of the time and the space, the wonders of the world that they brought to light and the sense of wonder with which they approached those worlds.

Notes

1 Richard William Southern, *The Making of the Middle Ages*, Yale: Yale University Press, 1962, p. 33.
2 Ibid.
3 *Medieval Sourcebook: Liutprand of Cremona: Report of His Mission to Constantinople*, Internet Medieval Sourcebook, Copyright Paul Halsall, January 1996. Accessed 27 October 2014.
4 I have discussed all this in detail in "Historiography and the Construction of a Communal Identity: Western Europe and India", published in *The ICFAI Journal of History and Culture*, 1.1, May 2007, pp. 56–72.
5 Cited in Evelyn Edson, The *World Map 1300–1492: The Persistence of Tradition and Transformation*, Baltimore: The Johns Hopkins University Press, 2007, p. 98.
6 Marcus N. Adler, *The Itinerary of Benjamin of Tudela, Critical Text, Translation and Commentary*, London: Oxford University Press, 1907, Introduction, p. x. Accessed through Project Gutenberg, 26 October 2014.
7 Donald Lach, *Asia in the Making of Europe*, Vol. II: *A Century of Wonder, Book Three: The Scholarly Disciplines*, Chicago: The University of Chicago Press, 1977, Paperback edition, 1994, p. 396. Book Two has on the cover a picture of a man on a camel and behind that an ox followed by a man carrying a stick, while Book 3 has a picture of Brama, Visno, and Hispar (Siva).
8 This may also be a reason for the lack of description in Rabban Sawma's account, mentioned earlier – they already knew the west, and didn't feel the need to know any more.
9 Ibid., Vol. 9, p. 24.
10 See Chapter 3.
11 Carpini, op. cit., p. 220.
12 Ibid., p. 237.
13 J. Tallboys Wheeler, *Early Travels in India: Reprints of Rare and Curious Narratives of Old Travellers in India, in the Sixteenth and Seventeenth Centuries*, London: Deep Publications (repr.), 1864, 1974, p. 72. Also William Foster (ed.), *Early Travels in India, 1583–1619*, London: Oxford University Press, 1921, reprinted 1968.
14 18th century French historian and Jesuit priest who wrote a book called *The History of the Mogul Dynasty* published in 1715 and based entirely on Manucci's work.
15 Ibid., p. 41.
16 See Romila Thapar, *Sakuntala*, New Delhi: Kali for Women, Second Impression, 2000.
17 Prof. Heiler, theologian, in 1932 – cited by Ronald Inden, *Imagining India*, Oxford: Basil Blackwell Ltd., 1990, p. 97.
18 Paul Carter, *The Road to Botany Bay: An Exploration of Landscape and History*, Minneapolis: University of Minnesota Press, 2010.

19 Cited by Ian J. Barrow, *Making History, Drawing Territory: British Mapping in India, c. 1756–1905*, Oxford: Oxford University Press, 2003, p. 11.
20 Shakespeare, *Othello*, Act II, Scene i.
21 See for example Edward Brooke-Hitching, *The Phantom Atlas: The Greatest Myths, Lies and Blunders on Maps*, London: Simon & Schuster, 2016, p. 179, where it is also pointed out that these imaginary creatures were conflated by Shakespeare with the Anthropophagi who were cannibals.
22 Simon Ryan, "The Cartographic Eye: Mapping and Ideology", *Sydney Open Journals Online*, 2013, pp. 13–18.

Select Bibliography

Adams, Percy G. 1962. *Travelers & Travel Liars 1660–1800*. Berkeley: University of California Press.
Adler, Marcus N. 1907. *The Itinerary of Benjamin of Tudela, Critical Text, Translation and Commentary*. London: Oxford University Press.
Alam, Muzaffar and Subrahmanyam, Sanjay. 2007. *Indo-Persian Travels in the Age of Discoveries, 1400–1800*. Cambridge: Cambridge University Press.
Arnold, David. 2005. *Tropics and the Travelling Gaze: India, Landscape and Science, 1800–1856*. New Delhi: Permanent Black.
Bacon, Francis. 2005. *Essays on Travaille*. New Delhi: Permanent Black.
Barbour, Richmond. 2009. *The Third Voyage Journals: Writings and Performance in the London East India Company, 1607–10*. Basingstoke: Palgrave Macmillan.
Beazley, Charles Raymond. 1903. *Voyages and Travels*. London: Archibald Constable & Co.
Beckingham, Charles Fraser and Hamilton, Bernard. 1996. *Prester John: The Mongols and the Ten Lost Tribes*. Aldershot: Variorum.
Brent-Dyer, Elinor M. 1929. *Chalet School Series*. London: Armada Books, Collins Publishing Group (1925–1970).
Brooke-Hitching, Edward. 2016. *The Phantom Atlas: The Greatest Myths, Lies and Blunders on Maps*. London: Simon & Schuster.
Bunyan, John. 1975. *The Pilgrim's Progress*, Edited by Roger Sharrock and J.B. Wharey. Oxford: Oxford University Press.
Burnell, Arthur Coke and Tiele, Pieter Anton (tr. and ed.). 1885, 1988. *The Voyage of John Huyghen van Linschoten to the East Indies*, 2 vols. London: Hakluyt Society; New Delhi: Asian Educational Services Reprint.
Burton, Richard (ed.). 1888. *The Book of One Thousand and One Nights*, Vol. 6, Stories of Sindbad the Sailor. London: The Burton Club.
Catrou, Francois. 1907. *The History of the Mogul Dynasty*. Banbasi Office.
Chaudhuri, Supriya. 2007. "The Idea of India", Paper presented (in Italian as L'Idea dell'India), at International Conference on Oriente e Occidente nel Rinascimento, XIX Convegno di Istituto Francesco Petrarca, Chianciano-Pienza, Italy, July.
Colber, Benjamin and Hambrook, Glyn. 2007. "Editors' Introduction", *Comparative Critical Studies*, 4.2.
Commissariat, Manekshah Sorabshah. 1938. *A History of Gujarat, Longmans*, Green & Co. Ltd.
Constable, Archibald (tr. and ed.). 1891, 1916, 1983. *Francois Bernier's Travels in Mogul Empire A.D. 1656–1666*, first published 1891, revised Vincent Smith. London: Oxford University Press; First Indian reprint, New Delhi: Oriental Books Reprint Corporation.

Select Bibliography

Crooke, William (ed.). 1909, 1992. *A New Account of East India and Persia, Being Nine Years Travel, 1672–1681, by John Fryer.* London: Chiswell; New Delhi: Asian Educational Services Reprint.

Dallmayr, Fred. 2001. *Beyond Orientalism: Essays on Cross-Cultural Encounter.* Jaipur: Rawat Publications (repr.).

Dames, Mansel Longworth (tr. and ed.). 1918–1821, 2002. *The Book of Duarte Barbosa*, 2 vols. London: Hakluyt Society; New Delhi: Asian Educational Services Second Reprint.

Danvers, Frederick Charles. 1894. *The Portuguese in India.* London: W. Allen & Co.

Denton, Andrew. 2012. "The Quest for Prester John", *Vexillum, the Undergraduate Journal of Classical and Medieval Studies*, Issue 2.

Dharampal (ed.). 1971. *Indian Sciences and Technology in the Eighteenth Century: Some Contemporary European Accounts.* New Delhi: Impex.

Edson, Evelyn. 2007. *The World Map 1300–1492: The Persistence of Tradition and Transformation.* Baltimore: The Johns Hopkins University Press.

Ellis, Sir Henry. 1825–1846. *Original Letters Illustrating English History*, 2nd Series. London: Harding, Triphook and Leonard.

Fawcett, Lady and Fawcett, Charles (tr. and ed.). 1990. *The Travels of the Abbé Carré in India and the near East, 1672–1674*, 2 Vols. New Delhi: Asian Educational Services (repr.).

Fisher, Michael (ed.). 2007. *Beyond the Three Seas: Travellers' Tales of the Mughal Orient.* Random House India.

Foley, Henry. 1875. *Records of the English Province of the Society of Jesus.* London: Burns and Oates.

Foster, William. 1899. *The Embassy of Sir Thomas Roe to India.* London: Hakluyt Society.

Foster, William (ed.). 1921, 1968. *Early Travels in India, 1583–1619.* London: Oxford University Press.

Foster, William (ed.). 1906–1927. *The English Factories in India.* Oxford: Clarendon Press.

Foster, William. 1933. *England's Quest of Eastern Trade.* London: A & C Black Ltd.

Grey, Edward (ed.). 1892, 1991. *The Travels of Pietro Della Valle in India*, 2 Vols. London: Hakluyt Society; New Delhi: Asian Educational Services Reprint (repr.).

Guéret-Laferté, Michèle. 2004. *De l'Inde: Les voyages en Asie de Niccolò De'Conti.* Belgium: Brepols.

Hakluyt, Richard. 1599. *Principal Navigations*, particularly Vols. 2 and 3. London: G. Bishop, R. Newberie and R. Barker.

Hamilton, Alexander. 1739, 1995. *A New Account of the East Indies: Being the Observations and Remarks o Capt. Alexander Hamilton, from the Year 1688 to 1723.* London and New Delhi: Asian Educational Services Reprint.

Herbert, Thomas. 1638. *Some Years Travels into Africa and Asia the Great, Especially Describing the Famous Empires of Persia and Industant: As also Divers Other Kingdoms in the Orientall Indies, and I'les Adjacent.* London: Jacob Blome and Richard Bishop.

Herodotus. 1996. *Histories, Book 3*, Wordsworth Classics of World Literature.

Howard, Clare. 1913. *English Travellers of the Renaissance.* New York and London: Bodley Head.

Inden, Ronald. 1990. *Imagining India.* Oxford: Basil Blackwell Ltd., 1990.

Jones, John Winter (tr.) and Badger, George Percy (ed.). 1863. *The Travels of Ludovico di Varthema in Egypt, Syria, Arabia Deserta and Arabia Felix, in Persia, India and Ethiopia, A.S. 1503–1508.* London: Hakluyt Society.

Khanmohamodi, Shirin A. 2013. *In Light of Another's Word: European Ethnography in the Middle Ages*. Philadelphia: University of Pennsylvania Press.

Lach, Donald F. 1965. *Asia in the Making of Europe*, Vol. 1. Chicago: University of Chicago Press.

Lach, Donald F. 1977. *Asia in the Making of Europe*, Vol. 2. Chicago: University of Chicago Press.

Lach, Donald F. 1993. *Asia in the Making of Europe*, Vol. 3. Chicago: University of Chicago Press.

Latham, Ronald (tr. and ed.). 1958. *Marco Polo: The Travels*. Penguin Books.

Lewis, Clive Staples. 1980. *Chronicles of Narnia*. London: Collins Paperbacks.

Locke, J. Courtney. 1930. *The First Englishmen in India*. London: Broadway House.

Marsden, William (tr. and ed.). 1818, 1931, 2003. *The Travels of Marco Polo, the Venetian*. London; revised with an Introduction by John Masefield. London: J.M. Dent and Sons Limited; New Delhi: Asian Educational Services Reprint.

Matar, Nabil (tr. and ed.). 2003. *In the Lands of the Christians: Arabic Travel Writing in the Seventeenth Century*. New York: Routledge.

Medieval Sourcebook: Liutprand of Cremona: Report of His Mission to Constantinople, Internet Medieval Sourcebook. Copyright Paul Halsall, January. 1996.

Miège, Guy. 1669. *A Relation of Three Embassies from His Sacred Majestie Charles II to the Great Duke of Muscovie, the King of Sweden, and the King of Denmark: Performed by the Right Honorable the Earle of Carlisle in the Years 1663 & 1664*. London: John Starkey. (accessed through ttps://quod.lib.umich.edu/e/eebo2/A50829.0001.001?view=toc on 20/6/19).

Moreland, William Harrison and Geyl, Pieter (tr. and ed.). 1925, 1972. *Jahangir's India: The Remonstrantie of Francisco Pelsaert*. Cambridge: W. Heffer & Sons Ltd.; Indian Edition, New Delhi: Idarah-I Adabiyat-I Delli.

Mukherjee, Rila. 2018. "The Strange History of Prester John across the Indian Ocean", *Asian Review of World History*, 6.2, 2018.

Mundy, Peter. 1914. *The Travels of Peter Mundy, in Europe and Asia, 1608–1667, Vol. II: Travels in Asia, 1628–1634*. London: Hakluyt Society.

Oaten, Edward Farley. 1909, 1991. *European Travellers in India During the Fifteenth, Sixteenth and Seventeenth Centuries*. London and New Delhi: Asian Educational Services Reprint.

O'Doherty, Marianne. 2013. *The Indies and the Medieval West: Thought, Report, Imagination (Medieval Voyaging)*. Brepols.

Phillips, Kim M. 2013. *Before Orientalism: Asian Peoples and Cultures in European Travel Writing, 1245–1510*. Philadelphia: Penn Press.

Plays of Shakespeare, particularly *The Two Gentlemen of Verona, the Merchant of Venice and Othello*, various editions.

Pollard, Alfred William (ed.). 1900. *The Travels of Sir John Mandeville, with Three Narratives in Illustration of It: The Voyage of Johannes de Plano Carpini, the Journal of William de Rubruquis, and the Journal of Friar Odoric from Hakluyt's "Navigations, Voyages and Discoveries"*. London: Macmillan & Co.

Prasad, Ram Chandra. 1965, rev ed. 1980. *Early English Travellers in India*. New Delhi: Motilal Banarsidass.

Purchas, Samuel. 1905. *Purchas His Pilgrimes*, particularly Vols. 2, 4 and 5. Glasgow: James Maclehose & Company.

Rawlinson, George (tr. and ed.), *Herodotus Histories*, Wordsworth Editions of World Literature, 1996.

Select Bibliography

Riley, J. Horton. 1899. *Ralph Fitch: England's Pioneer to India*. London: J. Fisher Unwin.

Roe, Sir Thomas and Fryer, Dr. John. 1873, 1993. *Travels in India in the Seventeenth Century*, reprinted from the "Calcutta Weekly Englishman". London: Turner and Co.; New Delhi: Asian Educational Services Reprint.

Ross, Sir E. Denison. 1926, 1968. "Prester John and the Empire of Ethiopia", Arthur P. Newton (ed.), *Travel and Travellers of the Middle Ages*. New York: Barnes & Noble.

Rubies, Joan-Pau. 2000. *Travel and Technology in the Renaissance: South India through European Eyes, 1250–1625*. Cambridge: Cambridge University Press, 2000.

Ryan, Simon. 2013. "The Cartographic Eye: Mapping and Ideology", *Sydney Open Journals Online*, 13–18. https://openjournals.library.sydney.edu.au/index.php/JASAL/article/view/9947

Seshan, Radhika. 2007. "Identity Formation, Foundational Myths and Communalism: Western Europe and India", *The ICFAI Journal of History and Culture*, 1, 1, May.

Seshan, Radhika. 2008. "Fabled Lands, Fabulous Wealth: Travel Accounts from the Fourteenth to the Eighteenth Century", unpublished paper, presented at the Conference on "On the Road: Writing Travel and Travellers", Jadavpur University, Kolkata, November.

Seshan, Radhika (ed.). 2014. *Convergences: Rethinking India's Past*. New Delhi: Primus Books.

Silverberg, Robert. 1972, 2001. *The Realm of Prester John*. Republished London: Phoenix Press.

Southern, Richard William. 1961. *The Making of the Middle Ages*. Yale: Yale University Press.

Starkey, Paul and Starkey, Janet (ed.). 2001. *Travellers in Egypt*. London: Tauris Parke Paperbacks.

Strabo, *Book XV, On India*. https://sourcebooks.fordham.edu/ancient/strabo-geog-book15-india.asp

Sykes, Percy (ed.). 1927. *Sir John Chardin's Travels in Persia*. London: The Argonaut Press.

Teltscher, Kate. 1997. *India Inscribed*. New Delhi: Oxford India Paperbacks.

Temple, Richard (ed.). 1914. *The Travels of Peter Mundy, in Europe and Asia 1608–1667, Vol. II, Travels in Asia 1628–1634*. London: Hakluyt Society.

Terry, Edward. 1655. *A Voyage to the East Indies*. London: J. Wilkie, S. Hayes, W. Cater and E. Easton.

Thapar, Romila. 2000. *Sakuntala*. New Delhi: Kali for Women, Second Impression.

Thompson, Carl (ed.). 2016. *The Routledge Companion to Travel Writing*. London: Routledge.

Ullendorff, Edward and Beckingham, Charles Fraser. 1982. *The Hebrew Letters of Prester John*. Oxford: Oxford University Press.

Van Duzer, Chet. 2014. *Sea Monsters on Medieval and Renaissance Maps*. The British Library.

Wallis Budge, E.A. (tr. and ed.). 1928. *The Monks of Kublai Khan, Emperor of China, or: The History of the Life and Travels of Rabban Sawma, Envoy and Plenipotentiary of the Mongol Khans to the Kings of Europe*. London: The Religious Tract Society.

102 Select Bibliography

Wheeler, J. Talboys (ed.). 1864, 1964. *Early Travels in India: Reprints of Rare and Curious Narratives of Old Travellers in India, in the Sixteenth and Seventeenth Centuries*. Calcutta: Englishman Press; New Delhi: Deep Publications reprint.

The World Displayed: Of, a Collection of Voyages and Travels Selected from the Writers of All Nations, in Eight Volumes, Travels of Sir John Chardin, Vol. 7. Philadelphia: Dobelbower, Key, and Simpson, 1795–1796.

Yule, Henry (tr. and ed.). 1863. *Mirabilia Descripta, the Wonders of the East, by Friar Jordanus (circa 1330)*. London: Hakluyt Society.

Yule, Henry (tr. and ed.). 1866. *Cathay and the Way Thither: Being a Collection of Medieval Notices of China*. London: Hakluyt Society.

Yule, Henry (tr. and ed.). 1903. *The Book of Ser Marco Polo, the Venetian*. London: J. Murray.

Index

20,000 Leagues under the Sea 5

Adams, Percy G. 5
Albuquerque 70, 72
Aleppo 49, 71
Alexander (King) 12, 18
Alexander III (Pope) 15
Alexander IV (Pope) 23
Antonio, Don 46
Arabic language 51
Aracan 49
Asia in the Making of Europe 5, 86
assassins 6
Avars 14

Bacon, Francis 71
Baghdad 26, 31
Ballagatte 48
Banks, Sir Joseph 76
baptisms 44
barbarians 28
Barbosa, Duarte 43–45
Basra 44, 49, 63
Batu Khan 23
Benjamin of Tudela 85
Benomotapa 53
Bernier, Francois 42, 60, 66, 72, 78, 83
al-Beruni 3
Beyond the Three Seas: Travellers' Tales from Mughal India 4
Black Sea 25, 29, 33, 34
Bowrey, Thomas 73, 74, 88
Bracciolini, Poggio 38, 39
Brahmins 42
Buchanan, Francis 76
Buddha 12
Buddhism 12
Buddhist pilgrims 3

Bunyan, John 6
Byzantium 13, 26, 28, 66, 83, 84

Caffaria 53
calcatix 35
Cambaya 43
Campa (Champa) 30
Canton 30
Cape of Good Hope 43, 56, 57, 75
Carpini, Johannes de Plano 23–25, 27, 28, 48, 89, 90
Carré, Abbé 63–65, 72
Carter, Paul 93
cartography 19
Catalan atlas 19
Cathay 18, 29, 34, 72
Catrou, François 90
Chaldaea 28
Chaldaeans 28
Chardin, Jean 75
Charybdis 34
China 13, 14, 16–18, 29, 32
Christa Purana 45
Christian Arabs 72
Christians 14, 15, 23, 26, 35, 44, 64, 72
Chulias 74
Cochin 71
colonialism 8, 45
Columbus 16
Columbus, Christopher 38
Comparative Critical Studies of 2007 3
Constantinople 31, 33, 66, 71
Conti, Nicolo 38–42, 86
Coryat, Thomas 47
Cosmas Indicopleustes 12
cotton 11
Cracurim [Karakorum] 24, 26
Cyprus 63, 85

Index

Darius 11
Dead Sea 30
Defoe, Daniel 19
della Valle, Pietro 51, 52, 58, 91

East India Company 46, 57, 58, 60, 73
Eldred, John 45
Emanuel I 14
Empire of Mogor 47
Eschenbach, Wolfram von 16
Ethiopia 53
Europeans 3, 4, 16, 18, 23, 25, 27, 30, 40, 60
European Travellers in India 3

fictional lands, maps 5
Finch, William 47
Fisher, Michael 4
Fitch, Ralph 5, 45–47, 52, 79, 91
Franks 40
Friar Odoric of Pordenone 28
friars 23, 27, 29, 38
Fryer, John 60–63, 73, 79

Ganges 35, 39, 46, 48
Gentiles 46, 51
Gentlemen's Magazine 5
Geographical Account of the Countries around the Bay of Bengal, 1659–1669, A 88
Geographical Account Of The Countries Round The Bay of Bengal, 1669–1679, A 74
Germany 16
Gombroon 71
Greeks 11, 92
Gulliver's Travels 5, 19

Hakluyt Voyage volumes 3
Hamilton, Alexander 74
Hamlet 79
Hawkins, William 47, 51, 54
Henry VI 70
Henry VIII 70
Herbert, Thomas 19, 51–53
Herodotus 11, 17
Hinduism 92
Hippolytus 84
Hirava 42
History of the Mongols 23
holocaust 22
Holy Land 14, 70
Huns 22

imagined lands 11–21
India Extra Gangem 31, 72
India Intra Gangem 31, 72
Indian commodities 88
Indians 11, 52, 53, 56, 57, 60, 62, 65, 72
Informacon for Pylgrymes unto the Holy Lande 70
Inland India 29
Innocent IV (Pope) 23
Iraq 26
Islam 13, 85

Jahangir 59, 91
Java 30, 32, 40, 48
John, Prester 5, 14–17, 19, 31, 32, 44, 85, 86
Jordanus 34, 35
Jourdain, John 73
Justinian 13

Kalyan port 12
Kanbalu 32
Keeling, William 78
Khan, Changez 22, 31, 32
Khan, Kublai 31, 77
Khanate 27, 28
kingdom of Mobar 29
Kipling, Rudyard 19
Kublai Khan's court 31

Lach, Donald 5, 86
Latin Christendom 13
Leedes, William 45
licentiousness, upper class 60
Linschoten, John Huyghen van 48, 89
Liutprand 84
Lombards 14
Lyons 23, 24

Magellan, Ferdinand 38
Magyars 22
Mahometans 48
Ma-huan 38
Mamelukes 41
Mandeville 18
Mandeville, Sir John 16
Mandeville's Travels 5
marauders 14
Martin, Francois 73
Mechua 42
Megasthenes 12
Melynde 43
Merchant of Venice 79

Methwold, William 73
Miège, Guy 7, 65, 66
Milinda Panho 12
Mirabilia 34
Mirabilia Descripta 34
Mogul court 46
Mombasa 43
Mongols 18, 23–28, 31, 42, 52, 85, 89–91; attacks 22; ferocity of 22; incursions 23; raids 22, 26
Monomotapa 53
monopolies 73
Moores 46
Mozambique 48
Mundy, Peter 55, 57–58, 61, 64, 73, 91
Muslims 26, 48, 53, 59, 64

Naeri 42
Nestorians 26
New Account of The East Indies from the years 1688 to 1723, A 74
Newberry, John 45
Nicephorus 84
Nicholas of Cusa 19
Nur Jahan 59, 60

Oaten, E.F. 3
Odoric, friar 28–31, 33–35, 39, 86, 89, 91
On Travaille 71
organisational structure, society 42
'Orient, The' 7, 8
Oriental Despot 91
Orientalism 7
Ormuz 29, 42, 44, 46, 48, 71
Orthodox Church 83
Othello 94

pagans 15, 42
pahars 58
Palermo 85
Paris, Mathew 85
Parossitae 25
Parsifal 16
Patna 46
Pegalotti 34, 41
Pegu 49
Pelsaert, Francisco 51, 59, 60, 62, 72
pepper 29, 30, 32
Persia 28, 31, 34, 46
Persian language 51
The Pilgrim's Progress 6

Poliar 42
Polo, Marco 16, 17, 19, 31, 32, 35, 83, 86
Portuguese 43; colonialism 40
Porus 29
prophetic religion 92

Quiloa 43
Quilon 35

religion 42, 62, 91
Renaissance 14, 38, 69, 71
Robinson Crusoe 5, 19
Roe, Thomas 51–55, 57, 72, 88
Rubruquis, William de 23, 25, 27, 28, 34, 52, 89, 90
Ryan, Simon 95

safar concept 6
Said, Edward 7
Saracens 14, 15, 28
Sawma, Rabban bar 77
science fiction 4
self-indulgence 1
self-realisation 6
Seljuks 26
Seres 13, 23
Shakespeare 94
Siam 49
Sindbad the Sailor 19, 79
Slav tribes 14
Sofala 43, 44
Sparta 12
St. Denis 26
Stephen, Father (Jesuit priest) 45
stereotypes 6, 79
Stevenson, R.L. 19
St. James of Compostella 70
stories 2, 3–4, 19; retelling 2
Story, James 45
storytelling 2
Strabo's geography 12
Sufi mystics 6
Surat 71
Swift, Jonathan 5, 19
Syria 26

Tabriz 34
Tai-Du 32
Tana 29, 33, 34
Tartars 28, 31
Tavernier, Jean-Baptiste 42, 73
Temple of the Mahometans 51

Index

Terry, Edward 51–53, 55, 56, 58, 72, 75, 87
Thapar, Romila 2
Theophylact Simocatta 12, 13
Third Voyage of the East India Company 78
Thracians 11
three Indias 14, 15, 31
Tiva 42
traveller's tale 2–3
travel lies 5
travelling minstrel 2
travel literature 3
travel narratives 1, 83
travelogues 3, 45, 69, 95; of Robinson Crusoe 4
Travels in the Mogul Empire 83
Travels of Marco Polo, The 1
Travels of Sir John Mandeville 16, 78
travel writing 2, 3
Treasure Island 19
tribes of Tartary 31
Troglodites 53
Tudor England 71

Turkish language 51
Turkomenia 31
Turks 15
Two Gentlemen of Verona, The 79

ubiquitous map 1
Un-khan 31

Vale Perilous 17
Van Duzer, Chet 19
Varthema, Ludovico di 6, 40–42, 45, 48, 58
Vasco da Gama 38, 70, 72
Verne, Jules 5
Vijayanagar 39

Wends 22
White Seal, The 19
Whittington, Nicholas 60, 90
William of Malmesbury 15
Worde, Wrykyn de 16

zambucos 44
Zheng-he 38